AWS Certified Security - Specialty

Practice Questions

Version 1

www.ipspecialist.net

Document Control

Proposal Name	:	AWS – Security - Specialty – Practice Questions
Document Version	:	1.0
Document Release Date	:	11th June - 2019
Reference	:	SCS – C01

Feedback:

If you have any comments regarding the quality of this book, or otherwise alter it to better suit your needs, you can contact us through email at info@ipspecialist.net

Please make sure to include the book title and ISBN in your message.

About IPSpecialist

IPSPECIALIST LTD. IS COMMITTED TO EXCELLENCE AND DEDICATED TO YOUR SUCCESS.

Our philosophy is to treat our customers like family. We want you to succeed, and we are willing to do anything possible to help you make it happen. We have the proof to back up our claims. We strive to accelerate billions of careers with great courses, accessibility, and affordability. We believe that continuous learning and knowledge evolution are most important things to keep re-skilling and up-skilling the world.

Planning and creating a specific goal is where IPSpecialist helps. We can create a career track that suits your vision as well as develop the competencies that you need to become a professional Network Engineer. We can also assist you with the execution and evaluation of proficiency level based on the career track you choose, as they are customized to fit your specific goals.

We help you STAND OUT from the crowd through our detailed IP training content packages.

Course Features:

❖ Self-Paced learning
  • Learn at your own pace and in your own time
❖ Covers Complete Exam Blueprint
  • Prep-up for the exam with confidence
❖ Case Study Based Learning
  • Relate the content with real life scenarios
❖ Subscriptions that suits you
  • Get more pay less with IPS Subscriptions
❖ Career Advisory Services
  • Let industry experts plan your career journey
❖ Virtual Labs to test your skills
  • With IPS vRacks, you can testify your exam preparations
❖ Practice Questions
  • Practice Questions to measure your preparation standards
❖ On Request Digital Certification
  • On request digital certification from IPSpecialist LTD

About the Authors:

This book has been compiled with the help of multiple professional engineers. These engineers specialize in different fields e.g Networking, Security, Cloud, Big Data, IoT etc. Each engineer develops content in its specialized field that is compiled to form a comprehensive certification guide.

About the Technical Reviewers:

Nouman Ahmed Khan

AWS-Architect, CCDE, CCIEX5 (R&S, SP, Security, DC, Wireless), CISSP, CISA, CISM is a Solution Architect, working with a major telecommunication provider in Qatar. He works with enterprises, mega-projects, and service providers to help them select the best-fit technology solutions. He also works closely as a consultant to understand customer business processes and helps select an appropriate technology strategy to support business goals. He has more than 14 years of experience working in Pakistan/Middle-East & UK. He holds a Bachelor of Engineering Degree from NED University, Pakistan, and M.Sc. in Computer Networks from the UK.

Abubakar Saeed

Abubakar Saeed has more than twenty-five years of experience, Managing, Consulting, Designing, and implementing large-scale technology projects, extensive experience heading ISP operations, solutions integration, heading Product Development, Presales, and Solution Design. Emphasizing on adhering to Project timelines and delivering as per customer expectations, he always leads the project in the right direction with his innovative ideas and excellent management.

Syed Hanif Wasti

Syed Hanif Wasti is a Computer science graduate working professionally as a Technical Content Developer. He is a part of a team of professionals operating in the E-learning and digital education sector. He holds a bachelor's degree in Computer Sciences from PAF-KIET, Pakistan. He has completed training of MCP and CCNA. He has both technical knowledge and industry sounding information, which he uses efficiently in his career. He was working as a Database and Network administrator, while having experience of software development.

Areeba Tanveer

Areeba Tanveer is working professionally as a Technical Content Developer. She holds Bachelor's of Engineering degree in Telecommunication Engineering from NED University of Engineering and Technology. She also worked as a project Engineer in Pakistan Telecommunication Company Limited (PTCL). She has both technical knowledge and industry sounding information, which she uses effectively in her career.

Afia Afaq

Afia Afaq works as a Technical Content Developer. She holds a Bachelor of Engineering Degree in Telecommunications Engineering from NED University of Engineering and Technology. She also has worked as an intern in Pakistan Telecommunication Company Limited (PTCL) as well as in Pakistan Meteorological Department (PMD). Afia Afaq uses her technical knowledge and industry sounding information efficiently in her career.

Hira Arif

Hira Arif is an Electrical Engineer, graduated from NED University of Engineering and Technology, working professionally as a Technical Content Writer. Prior to that, she worked as a Trainee Engineer at Sunshine Corporation. She utilizes her knowledge and technical skills profoundly when required.

Muhammad Yousuf

Muhammad Yousuf is a professional technical content writer. He is Cisco Certified Network Associate in Routing and Switching and EC - Council Certified Ethical Hacker, holding bachelor's degree in Telecommunication Engineering from Sir Syed University of Engineering and Technology. He has both technical knowledge and industry sounding information, which he uses perfectly in his career.

Free Resources:

With each workbook you buy from Amazon, IPSpecialist offers free resources to our valuable customers.

Once you buy this book you will have to contact us at support@ipspecialist.net or tweet @ipspecialistnet to get this limited time offer without any extra charges.

Free Resources Include:

Exam Practice Questions in Quiz Simulation: IP Specialists' Practice Questions have been developed keeping in mind the certification exam perspective. The collection of these questions from our technology workbooks is prepared to keep the exam blueprint in mind covering not only important but necessary topics as well. It is an ideal document to practice and revise your certification.

Career Report: This report is a step by step guide for a novice who wants to develop his/her career in the field of computer networks. It answers the following queries:

- Current scenarios and future prospects
- Is this industry moving towards saturation or are new opportunities knocking at the door?
- What will the monetary benefits be?
- Why to get certified?
- How to plan and when will I complete the certifications if I start today?
- Is there any career track that I can follow to accomplish specialization level?

Furthermore, this guide provides a comprehensive career path towards being a specialist in the field of networking and also highlights the tracks needed to obtain certification.

Our Products

Technology Workbooks

IPSpecialist Technology workbooks are the ideal guides to developing the hands-on skills necessary to pass the exam. Our workbook covers official exam blueprint and explains the technology with real life case study based labs. The content covered in each workbook consists of individually focused technology topics presented in an easy-to-follow, goal-oriented, step-by-step approach. Every scenario features detailed breakdowns and thorough verifications to help you completely understand the task and associated technology.

We extensively used mind maps in our workbooks to visually explain the technology. Our workbooks have become a widely used tool to learn and remember the information effectively.

vRacks

Our highly scalable and innovative virtualized lab platforms let you practice the IP Specialist Technology Workbook at your own time and your own place as per your convenience.

Quick Reference Sheets

Our quick reference sheets are a concise bundling of condensed notes of the complete exam blueprint. It is an ideal handy document to help you remember the most important technology concepts related to certification exam.

Practice Questions

IP Specialists' Practice Questions are dedicatedly designed for certification exam perspective. The collection of these questions from our technology workbooks are prepared to keep the exam blueprint in mind covering not only important but necessary topics as well. It is an ideal document to practice and revise your certification.

AWS Certifications

AWS Certifications are industry-recognized credentials that validate your technical cloud skills and expertise while assisting in your career growth. These are one of the most valuable IT certifications right now since AWS has established an overwhelming lead in the public cloud market. Even with the presence of several tough competitors such as Microsoft Azure, Google Cloud Engine, and Rackspace, AWS is by far the dominant public cloud platform today, with an astounding collection of proprietary services that continues to grow.

The two key reasons as to why AWS certifications are prevailing in the current cloud-oriented job market:

- There is a dire need for skilled cloud engineers, developers, and architects – and the current shortage of experts is expected to continue into the foreseeable future
- AWS certifications stand out for their thoroughness, rigor, consistency, and appropriateness for critical cloud engineering positions

Value of AWS Certifications

AWS places equal emphasis on sound conceptual knowledge of its entire platform as well as on hands-on experience with the AWS infrastructure and its many unique and complex components and services.

For Individuals

- Demonstrate your expertise to design, deploy, and operate highly available, cost-effective, and secure applications on AWS
- Gain recognition and visibility for your proven skills and proficiency with AWS
- Earn tangible benefits such as access to the AWS Certified LinkedIn Community, invite to AWS Certification Appreciation Receptions and Lounges, AWS Certification Practice Exam Voucher, Digital Badge for certification validation, AWS Certified Logo usage, access to AWS Certified Store
- Foster credibility with your employer and peers

For Employers

- Identify skilled professionals to lead IT initiatives with AWS technologies
- Reduce risks and costs to implement your workloads and projects on the AWS platform

- Increase customer satisfaction

Types of Certification

Role-Based Certifications:
- **Foundational** - Validates overall understanding of the AWS Cloud. Prerequisite to achieving Specialty certification or an optional start towards Associate certification
- **Associate** - Technical role-based certifications. No prerequisite
- **Professional** - Highest level technical role-based certification. Relevant Associate certification required

Specialty Certifications:
- Validate advanced skills in specific technical areas
- Require one active role-based certification

About AWS Certified Security - Specialty Exam

Exam Questions	Multiple choice and multiple answer
Time to Complete	170 minutes
Available Languages	English, Japanese, Korean, Simplified Chinese
Exam Reference Number	SCS – C01
Exam Fee	300 USD

The AWS Certified Security – Specialty exam validates advanced technical skills and experience in securing the AWS platform. Example concepts you should understand for this exam include:

➢ Understanding of specialized data classification and AWS data protection mechanisms
➢ Understanding of data encryption methods and AWS mechanisms to implement them
➢ Understanding of secure Internet protocols and AWS mechanisms to implement them

- Working knowledge of AWS security services and features of services to provide a secure production environment
- Understanding of security operations and risk
- Ability to make trade-off decisions with regard to cost, security, and deployment complexity given a set of application requirements
- Competency gained from two or more years of production deployment experience using AWS security services and features

Recommended AWS Knowledge

- Minimum five years of IT security experience designing and implementing security solutions
- At least two years of hands-on experience securing AWS workloads
- Security controls for workloads on AWS

	Domain	%
Domain 1	Incident Response	12%
Domain 2	Logging & Monitoring	20%
Domain 3	Infrastructure Security	26%
Domain 4	Identity and Access Management	20%
Domain 5	Data Protection	22%
Total		100%

Practice Questions

1. You are developing an application which will use Kinesis stream. The stream will be encrypted using the KMS keys. Upon conducting a load test with around 1500 requests per second; requests were throttled. What could be the reason for it?
   A. The number of streams has a limit
   B. There is a limit on KMS API calls
   C. You can only have 100 shards with 10 records processed per shard
   D. AWS Kinesis only allows 1000 records to be read per second

2. The data streams generated by your application are going to be processed by Lambda functions. Which of the two requirements ensure that Kinesis could work with Lambda? (Choose 2)
   A. Use the AWSLambdaKinesisExecutionRole
   B. Use the AWSLambdaExecutionRole
   C. Create a service role of the type AWS Lambda
   D. Create a service role of the type AWS Kinesis

3. You are planning to use Kinesis Data Firehose. The data will be sent to S3 bucket and will be encrypted at rest using a KMS key. Which of the following permissions should be there in the policy attached to Kinesis Data Firehose? (Choose 2)
   A. Kms:Encrypt
   B. Kms:Decrypt
   C. Kms:GenerateDataKey
   D. Kms:GenerateCustomerKey

4. The development team in your company is planning to use KCL library for an application. They have started development and accessing the streams using their IAM access keys. But the library keeps on throwing errors of being unable to perform stream related functions. What could be the issue?
   A. Make sure that the access keys have access to CloudWatch
   B. Ensure that the access keys have access to AWS Kinesis
   C. Make sure that the policy applied to the users has access to SQS and CloudWatch
   D. Ensure that the policy applied to the users has access to DynamoDB and CloudWatch

5. You are developing an application for your company which uses AWS Kinesis stream. According to company policy, all stored data must be encrypted at rest. How can you accomplish this in the easiest way possible?
   A. Enable server-side encryption for Kinesis streams
   B. Use AWS CLI to encrypt the data
   C. Use the SDK for Kinesis to encrypt the data before being stored at rest
   D. Enable client-side encryption for Kinesis streams

6. In your company, there are several applications running on EC2 instances with access to Kinesis streams via IAM roles. For security compliance, it is required to track the calls made to create Kinesis streams within the Kinesis service. What could be done to achieve this?
   A. Use CloudWatch metrics
   B. Use the Kinesis API tracker
   C. Use CloudTrail logs
   D. Write code to log the calls to a separate S3 bucket

7. Your company has several applications that are built on EC2 instances. EC2 instances access the Kinesis streams via IAM roles. The security policy enforces that the metrics should be recorded for streams at the shard level. How can this be done?
   A. Enable enhanced monitoring for the stream
   B. Use the basic monitoring available in CloudWatch
   C. Use DynamoDB for storing the logs
   D. Use CloudTrail logs

8. You are going to deploy an application on an EC2 instance. The application needs to access Kinesis Data Streams. There is a security mandate that no data should leave the VPC onto the internet. How will you ensure that the application complies with the security requirement?
   A. Use a VPC endpoint interface
   B. Use VPC endpoint gateway
   C. Use NAT gateway
   D. Enable VPC enhanced routing

9. You need to develop an application using Kinesis Analytics. The application will read records from Kinesis Data Streams. Which of the following actions are needed to be a part of the permission policy? (Choose 3)

A. Kinesis:GetShardIterator
B. Kinesis:DescribeStream
C. Kinesis:GetRecords
D. Kinesis:PutRecords

10. You need to develop an application using Kinesis streams. Which permissions should be given to the producers of the streams? (Choose 2)
    A. GetRecord
    B. PutRecord
    C. GetStream
    D. DescribeStream

11. Your team of developers is planning to use AWS Systems Manager to store parameters and encrypt these parameters using KMS. There is the need of a policy to ensure the retrieval of the keys. Which of the following would you define in the IAM policy? (Choose 2)
    A. Allow permission for kms:Encrypt
    B. Allow permission for kms:Decrypt
    C. Allow permissions to ssm:PutParameter
    D. Allow permissions to ssm:GetParameter

12. You have a set of files that are required to be encrypted at the client side. Your organization is already familiar with AWS, so you decided to use KMS to encrypt these files. Which of the following are the basic steps to be followed in the encryption process? (Choose 2)
    A. Import the key material while creating the CMK
    B. Use the CMK key to encrypt the files
    C. Create a new CMK in AWS KMS
    D. Use the data key to encrypt the files

13. Being the security administrator of your company, you are required to manage the CMK keys for your company's account. You have been requested to create alias for keys. Which of the following do you need to be aware of while creating alias keys?
    A. The alias key must be unique in the AWS account and AZ
    B. An alias key can point to multiple CMK keys at a time
    C. Each CMK key can have multiple alias' point to it

D. The alias key must be unique in the AWS account and region

14. You have to set the key policies for a set of users for a set of CMK keys. These users are developers who need to have the ability to encrypt and decrypt data using CMK keys. In your opinion, what is the minimum set of permissions that should be applied in the key policies?
    A. Allow actions on kms:Encrypt, kms:Decrypt, kms:ReEncrypt*, kms:GenerateDataKey*, kms:Create*
    B. Allow actions on kms:Encrypt, kms:Decrypt, kms:ReEncrypt*, kms:GenerateDataKey*
    C. Allow actions on kms:Encrypt, kms:Decrypt, kms:ReEncrypt*
    D. Allow actions on kms:Encrypt, kms:Decrypt, kms:ReEncrypt*, kms:GenerateDataKey*, kms:DescribeKey

15. Your company's application is hosted on a set of EC2 instances that are located in a private subnet. The application is required to use AWS KMS. How can this be done in the most secure way?
    A. Attach a NAT gateway to the VPC and convert the subnet to a public subnet
    B. Create a VPC endpoint interface and make the application use the VPC gateway
    C. Create a VPC endpoint gateway and make the application use the VPC gateway
    D. Attach an internet gateway to the VPC and convert the subnet to a public subnet

16. You are planning to encrypt the underlying data of your organization using AWS KMS. It is required to use your own key material to prove the ownership when it comes to the auditing of keys. Which of the following should be done in order to fulfill this requirement?
    A. Rotate the keys being used
    B. Disable the keys being used
    C. Use CloudTrail logs to see all the keys that have been used
    D. Use AWS Config to see where all the keys have been used

17. An organization excessively uses AWS KMS service and has defined a number of CMK keys. You need to provide a solution for a requirement; they want to get notified about any request made with the root user to create a key in the KMS service. How can this be done? (Choose 2)
    A. Use SNS to send notifications

B. Use SQS to send notifications

C. Use CloudWatch metrics for monitoring the API usage

D. Use CloudTrail service for monitoring the API usage

18. For experiments, you have been using KMS keys. You have created several CMK keys and have used them in applications in different areas. Which of the following is the best way to delete the keys that are not in use anymore? (Choose 2)

A. Rotate the keys being used

B. Disable the keys that are not being used

C. Use CloudTrail logs to see where all the keys have been used

D. Use AWS Config to see where all the keys have been used

19. You are using KMS heavily in your organization. You have a number of CMK keys. The management wants to be notified whenever a rotation of key is carried out. To get this done, which of the following should you choose?

A. Use the logs in AWS KMS

B. Use the AWS key policy

C. Use Trusted Advisor

D. Use CloudWatch events

20. Your company needs to host an application on an EC2 instance. The application will interact with a DynamoDB table. The security requirements state that all the data in DynamoDB table must be encrypted at rest. How can you do this with the least number of steps ensuring that all the data is encrypted?

A. Enable encryption at rest for the DynamoDB table. Then enable encryption of underlying keys and indexes

B. Enable encryption at rest for the DynamoDB table. Then enable encryption of underlying keys

C. Enable encryption at rest for the DynamoDB table. Then enable encryption of underlying indexes

D. Enable encryption at rest for the DynamoDB table

21. You are hosting your organization's web application behind a load balancer, and you have planned to use WAF to protect the application from web layer attacks. You need to initially get detailed information about the requests that get logged in the WAF service. How will you fulfill this requirement? (Choose 2)

A. Place a CloudFront distribution behind the ELB
B. Use AWS Kinesis Firehose service
C. Use WAF logs to store the information in the requests
D. Have an S3 bucket in place for log storage

22. You have planned to use WAF to protect your company's web application from various sorts of attacks. It is required to prevent traffic coming from a specific country. How would you do this?
    A. Create a Regex Match Condition
    B. Create a String Match Condition
    C. Create a Geographic Match Condition
    D. Create an IP Match Condition

23. You are planning to host an application on a fleet of EC2 instances. The database of the application will be on an RDS instance. Which of the following do you need, to ensure WAF integration with this structure? (Choose 2)
    A. Place a CloudFront distribution in front of the database instance
    B. Place a CloudFront distribution in front of the EC2 instances
    C. Place a Classic Load Balancer in front of the EC2 instances
    D. Place an Application Load Balancer in front of the EC2 instances

24. Your company is going to host their web application on AWS behind an application load balancer. The IT security team needs to respond to possible layer 7 DDoS attacks in the most efficient time possible. Which of the following will be helpful in achieving this? (Choose 2)
    A. Use AWS Shield service and contact AWS Support
    B. Use Network ACLs to absorb the traffic
    C. Pay for AWS Shield Advanced service and contact AWS Support Center
    D. Use the WAF service and set up rules to respond to such attacks

25. You have hosted an application behind an Application load balancer. The application will be placed behind the AWS WAF service. The application needs to abide by the PCI compliance standards. Which of the following would you choose to meet this requirement?
    A. Ensure to use the AWS Config as well
    B. Ensure to use the CloudFront distribution as well

C. Ensure to pay the AWS Advanced Shield Service

D. Consider buying a customized set of rules from the AWS Marketplace

26. A team has set up a CloudFront distribution with a web application hosted on an EC2 instance as the origin point. The security requirement mandates that all the configuration changes to the CloudFront distribution need to be recorded. Which of the following would you choose?

A. AWS CloudWatch

B. AWS CloudTrail

C. AWS Trusted Advisor

D. AWS Config

27. Your team has set up a CloudFront distribution with an application as origin point, which is hosted on an EC2 instance. The application serves videos to a number of users. There is a requirement to ensure that a certain section of files should only be accessible by a certain subscriber. Which of the following would you use to fulfill this requirement?

A. Use Lambda@Edge

B. Implement CORS

C. Use Signed cookies

D. Use pre-signed URLs

28. An application is hosted on EC2 instances which are being used as the original point for a CloudFront distribution. A security requirement is needed to ensure that all requests via CloudFront should be recorded. Which of the following steps would you carry out to achieve this? (Choose 2)

A. Store the logs on the EBS volume

B. Create a new trail in CloudTrail

C. Create a destination S3 bucket for the logs

D. Enable logging for the distribution

29. You are planning to use a CloudFront distribution to serve the objects in your S3 bucket to users across the globe. Assurance is required that the users only get to access the objects via CloudFront URLs. How would you assure this? (Choose 2)

A. Change the permissions on the bucket for the origin access identity has read permissions

B. Change the permissions on the bucket for the IAM users to have read permissions

C. Create an IAM user with the desired Access Keys

D. Create an origin access identity

30. To serve objects to users around the world, you are planning to use a CloudFront distribution. You want secure communication, and you want to use your own domain with CloudFront as distribution. How would you plan the implementation? (Choose 2)

A. Apply CORS for the distribution

B. Use KMS keys

C. Use an SSL certificate

D. Change the viewer protocol policy

31. Your organization is planning to move their on-premise workload to AWS. There is a plan of setting up own Active Directory setup on EC2 instances. They need to ensure that for the time being, resources from their on-premise data center can access the Active Directory setup. Which of the following should be done? (Choose 2)

A. Ensure that the AD connector is in place

B. Ensure that the security groups have been set for allowing traffic

C. Ensure that VPC flow logs have been enabled

D. Ensure that the network ACLs have been set for allowing traffic

32. You have set up AWS managed MS AD for your organization. There is a requirement that users who are being authenticated should use an extra security layer for authentication. How can this be achieved?

A. Enable MFA for the IAM users

B. Use access keys along with the username and passwords

C. Enable MFA for your AWS managed MS AD

D. Allow users to log in with their username and password

33. Your company has set up an AWS managed MS AD service. Assurance is required that user accounts should get locked after a specified number of failed login attempts. How can this be done?

A. Use IAM policies

B. Enable MFA for the directory service

C. Use password policies in the directory service

D. Enable LDAP over SSL

34. A company is migrating its workload to cloud and wants to set up their own Active Directory setup on EC2 instances. You are required to ensure that the administrators can securely access without the need to traverse through the internet. How would you ensure that?
    A. Provision a VPN connection
    B. Use the Remote Desktop Gateway
    C. Provision a NAT gateway in the public subnet
    D. Use DirectConnect

35. Your company has set up the AWS Managed MS AD. There are on-premise nodes that will be using the AWS Managed MS AD for authentication. You need to ensure that all traffic is encrypted in transit. How can you achieve this in the ideal manner?
    A. Enable server-side encryption
    B. Enable LDAP over HTTPS
    C. Enable LDAP over SSL
    D. Use KMS keys to encrypt the traffic

36. An organization has a client that needs an AWS web application. MySQL must be used as a database, and it should not be hosted in the cloud but in the data center of the client because of the security risks of that database. Which of the following solutions would ensure that the requirements of the customer get fulfilled?
    A. Build the application server on a public subnet and build the database in a private subnet with a secure SSH connection to the private subnet from the client's data center
    B. Build the application server on a public subnet and the database on a private subnet with a NAT instance between them
    C. Use the public subnet for the application server and use RDS with a storage gateway to access and synchronize the data securely from the local data center
    D. Build the application server on a public subnet and the database at the client's data center. Connect them with a VPN connection which uses IPsec

37. How do you assign permission to external AWS accounts on S3 bucket in your account? (choose any 2)
    A. Bucket policies
    B. Buckets ACL's

C. IAM users

D. IAM policies

38. A company has hired a security auditor from another company, and the auditor needs read-only access to AWS resources and logs of all AWS VPC records and events. How can the company fulfill the requirements of the auditors without compromising security in the cloud environment?

A. The company should contact AWS as part of the shared responsibility model, and AWS will grant required access to the third-party auditor.

B. Create an SNS notification that sends the CloudTrail log files to the auditor's email when CloudTrail delivers the logs to S3 but does not allow the auditor access to the AWS environment.

C. Enable CloudTrail logging and create an IAM user who has read-only permissions to the required AWS resources, including the bucket containing the CloudTrail logs.

D. Create a role that has the required permissions for the auditor

39. Your company has designed a web application with the requirement that users of the application get to sign in via external ID provider like Google, Facebook. How would they use AWS service for authentication?

A. AWS Config

B. AWS IAM

C. AWS SAML

D. AWS Cognito

40. You have created an AWS account. Now, you are worried that if root access is enabled, it might cause some issues. How would you mitigate the issues if the account has root access enabled? (choose any 2)

A. Delete the root access keys

B. Change the password for the root account

C. Create an Admin IAM user with the necessary permissions

D. Delete the root access account

41. From the following options, what is the responsibility of the customer? (choose any 2)

A. Decommissioning of old storage devices

B. Management of the Edge locations

C. Protection of data in transit

D. Encryption of data at rest

42. An enterprise manages its customer keys via AWS KMS. But with time, the existing keys are deleted as part of housekeeping. During the deletion how can they confirm that the key is no longer in use?

A. Use Key policies to see the access level for the keys

B. Change the IAM policy for the keys to see if other services are using the keys

C. Use CloudTrail to see if any KMS API request has been issued against existing keys

D. Rotate the keys once before deletion to see if other services are using the keys

43. How does a company perform monitoring and inspection of all the traffic packets of EC2 instances to identify the security threats? (choose any 2)

A. Use Network Access control lists logging

B. Use a host-based intrusion detection system

C. Use VPC Flow logs

D. Use a third party firewall installed on a central EC2 Instance

44. You have a set of EC2 instances behind an ELB in your company. A legacy protocol communicates certain applications hosted in such instances. There is a security mandate to secure all traffic between the customer and the EC2 instances. How would you meet the requirement?

A. Use a Classic load balancer and terminate the SSL connection at the EC2 Instances

B. Use an Application load balancer and terminate the SSL connection at the EC2Instances

C. Use a Classic load balancer and terminate the SSL connection at the ELB

D. Use an application load balancer and terminate the SSL connection at the ELB

45. The deployment of a critical application on AWS is your responsibility. Compliance of the controls laid down for this application to comply with PCI is part of the requirements for this application. Web application logs must also be monitored to identify malicious activities. To meet this requirement, which of the following services can be used? (Choose any 2)

A. Amazon CloudTrail

B. Amazon CloudWatch Logs

C. AWS Config

D. Amazon VPC Flow Logs

46. An employee continues to terminate EC2 cases in the production environment. The best way to ensure that this should not be done is to add an extra defense layer against termination. What is the best way to ensure that employees do not end the instances of production? (choose any 2)

   A. Modify the IAM policy on the user to require MFA before deleting EC2 instances

   B. Tag the instance with a production-identifying tag and modify the employee's group to allow only start, stop, and reboot API calls and not the terminate instance call.

   C. Modify the IAM policy on the user to require MFA before deleting EC2 instances and disable MFA access to the employee

   D. Tag the instance with a production-identifying tag and add resource-level permissions to the employee user with an explicit deny on the terminate API call to instances with the production tag.

47. There is a hybrid environment for your company with on-site servers and AWS servers. You plan for the server patching using the Systems Manager. Which of the following is a precondition for this?

   A. Ensure that an IAM Group is created for the on-premise servers

   B. Ensure that an IAM User is created

   C. Ensure that an IAM service role is created

   D. Ensure that the on-premise servers are running on Hyper-V

48. The DDoS assault usually targets web applications with lower traffic volumes compared to infrastructure assaults in the application layer. You may want to have WAF (Web Application Firewall) as part of your infrastructure to mitigate these types of attacks. WAFs are in line with your application traffic to inspect all HTTP requests. Sadly, this creates a scenario in which WAFs may become a fault point or a bottleneck. You need the ability to operate multiple WAFs on demand during traffic spikes to alleviate this problem. This type of WAF scaling is done through a "WAF sandwich." What is best described in the following statements as a "WAF sandwich?"

   A. The EC2 instance running your WAF software is included in an Auto Scaling group and placed in between two Elastic Load balancers

B. The EC2 instance running your WAF software is placed between your public subnets and your private subnets

C. The EC2 instance running your WAF software is placed between your public subnets and your Internet Gateway

D. The EC2 instance running your WAF software is placed between your private subnets and any NATed connections to the Internet

49. You have just developed a new mobile application, which handles large-scale data sets stored in Amazon Redshift analytical workloads. Therefore, Amazon Redshift tables are needed for the application. In practical and in security terms, which of the following methods would be best for accessing tables?

A. Use roles that allow a web identity federated user to assume a role that allows access to the RedShift table by providing temporary credentials

B. Create a RedShift read-only access policy in IAM and insert those credentials in the application

C. Create an HSM client certificate in Redshift and authenticate using this certificate

D. Create an IAM user and generate encryption keys for that user. Create a policy for RedShift read-only access. Embed the keys in the application.

50. How do you track access request of specific S3 bucket?

A. Enable AWS Config for the S3 bucket

B. Enable CloudWatch logs for the bucket

C. Enable CloudWatch metrics for the bucket

D. Enable server access logging for the bucket

51. How can you make your data encrypted in transit for connection with RDS instance?

A. Data Keys from CloudHSM

B. Data keys from AWS KMS

C. SSL from your application

D. Transparent data encryption

52. An organization uses EBS volumes in AWS, and for security purpose, they want all volumes to be encrypted and they want to get notified about any unencrypted volume in the account. How can this be done?

A. Use AWS Lambda to check for the unencrypted EBS volumes

B. Use AWS Guard duty to check for the unencrypted EBS volumes

C. Use AWS Config to check for unencrypted EBS volumes
D. Use AWS Inspector to inspect all the EBS volumes

53. You have a setup in which you use logging enabled S3 buckets. If changes to the S3 bucket are made, a config rule will be checked. If logging is deactivated, a function of Lambda is invoked. The Lambda function again allows the S3 bucket to log in. The whole flow is now a problem. You have checked the invoking of the Lambda function. However, the Lambda function does not re-open when logging for the bucket is disabled. Which one of the following might be a problem?
    A. You need to also use the API gateway to invoke the lambda function
    B. The AWS Lambda function should use Node.js instead of python
    C. The AWS Lambda function does not have appropriate permissions for the bucket
    D. The AWS Config rule is not configured properly

54. An organization uses EC2 instances, and they have compromised instances. They have strict policies and want to find out the culprit of the security breach. How would they do this? (choose any 3)
    A. Make sure that logs are stored securely for auditing and troubleshooting purpose
    B. Ensure that all access keys are rotated
    C. Isolate the machine from the network
    D. Ensure all passwords for all IAM users are changed
    E. Take a snapshot of the EBS volume

55. How does the data forwarded to S3 can be encrypted at rest?
    A. Enable MFA on the S3 bucket
    B. Enable server-side encryption on the S3 bucket
    C. Use SSL certificates to encrypt the data
    D. Use AWS Access keys to encrypt the data

56. An enterprise has its AWS account in which it hosts the resources. All API activities in all regions must be monitored. The audit must also be carried out in future regions. To meet this requirement, which of the following could be used?
    A. Create a Cloudtrail for each region. Use AWS Config to enable the trail for all future regions.

B. Create a Cloudtrail for each region. Use Cloudformation to enable the trail for all future regions.

C. Ensure one Cloudtrail trail is enabled for all regions

D. Ensure Cloudtrail for each region. Then enable for each future region.

57. A company is planning to use AWS for hosting the resources. They have multiple independent departments that also want to use AWS. Which of the following methods could be used to manage the accounts?

A. Use multiple AWS accounts, each account for each department

B. Use multiple IAM roles, each group for each department

C. Use multiple VPC's in the account, each VPC for each department

D. Use multiple IAM groups, each group for each department

58. From the following options, which is best to view event logs of all API on AWS which is read-only access to the auditor?

A. Configure the CloudTrail service in each AWS account and enable consolidated logging inside of CloudTrail

B. Configure the CloudTrail service in each AWS account, and have the logs delivered to an AWS bucket on each account, while granting the auditor permissions to the bucket via roles in the secondary accounts and a single primary IAM account that can assume a read-only role in the secondary AWS accounts

C. Configure the CloudTrail service in each AWS account and have the logs delivered to a single AWS bucket in the primary account and grant the auditor access to that single bucket in the primary account

D. Configure the CloudTrail service in the primary AWS account and configure consolidated billing for all the secondary accounts. Then grant the auditor access to the S3 bucket that receives the CloudTrail log files

59. An organization has an application in which it has multiple types of users like some have read-only access, or others have contributor access. The application is using AWS Cognito for authenticating. How would they manage the users?

A. Create different Cognito groups, one for the readers and the other for the contributors

B. This needs to be managed via Web security tokens

C. Create different Cognito endpoints, one for the readers and the other for the contributors

D. You need to manage this within the application itself

60. An enterprise uses Linux EC2 instance in AWS, and they want secure authentication to the instance from Windows. How can this requirement be met?
   A. Ensure the password is passed securely using SSL
   B. Ensure to create a strong password for logging into the EC2 Instance
   C. Use the private key to log into the instance
   D. Create a key pair using putty

61. An organization is using AWS resource for its infrastructure, and now they are searching for the security aspect of their CI / CD pipeline. They want to ensure that there should not be any high-security vulnerabilities in the EC2 instances. They also want to make sure that the DevSecOps process is complete. How can they meet this requirement?
   A. Use AWS Security Groups to ensure no vulnerabilities are present
   B. Use AWS Trusted Advisor API's in the pipeline for the EC2 Instances
   C. Use AWS Inspector API's in the pipeline for the EC2 Instances
   D. Use AWS Config to check the state of the EC2 instance for any sort of security issues

62. How will you make sure that your S3 bucket on AWS is only accessible via VPC endpoint?
   A. Modify the IAM Policy for the bucket to allow access for the VPC endpoint
   B. Modify the bucket Policy for the bucket to allow access for the VPC endpoint
   C. Modify the security groups for the VPC to allow access to the S3 bucket
   D. Modify the route tables to allow access for the VPC endpoint

63. An enterprise uses AWS to host its infrastructure on AWS EC2 instances. The EC2 instances are subjected to strict security regulations. You need a quick investigation of the underlying EC2 instance during a possible security violation. Which service can help you provide a test environment for the violated case quickly?
   A. AWS Config
   B. AWS CloudTrail
   C. AWS CloudFormation
   D. AWS CloudWatch

64. You have a huge number of keys specified in AWS KMS. You have an application which uses the keys very frequently. How can the cost of access keys in AWS KMS service be reduced?
    A. Use the right key policy
    B. Create an alias of the key
    C. Use Data key caching
    D. Enable rotation of the keys

65. An organization has one compromised EC2 instance. Which of the following steps are needed for applying digital forensics on the instance? (choose any 2)
    A. Create a separate forensic instance
    B. Terminate the instance
    C. Ensure that the security groups only allow communication to this forensic instance
    D. Remove the role applied to the Ec2 Instance

66. There is a set of AWS-hosted applications, database, and web servers. Behind an ELB, the web servers are located. The application, database and web servers have separate security groups. The security groups of the network were defined with some configuration. Contact between the application and database servers is problematic. What ideal set of MINIMAL steps would you take to resolve the problems between only the application and the database server?
    A. Check the Outbound security rules for the database security group, check both the Inbound and Outbound security rules for the application security group
    B. Check both the Inbound and Outbound security rules for the database security group, check the Inbound security rules for the application security group
    C. Check the Outbound security rules for the database security group, check the Inbound security rules for the application security group
    D. Check the Inbound security rules for the database security group, check the Outbound security rules for the application security group

67. Your development team needs to use AWS Lambda service for running multiple scripts, and now they need to understand the errors encountered during the running of the script. How can they do this?
    A. Use Cloudtrail to monitor for errors
    B. Use the AWS Inspector service to monitor for errors
    C. Use CloudWatch metrics and logs to watch for errors
    D. Use the AWS Config service to monitor for errors

68. In AWS Public Cloud the client has an RHEL Linux instance. The VPC and subnet used to host the instance that were created with the Network Access Control Lists default settings. You must provide secure access to the underlying instance for the IT Administrator. How can this be done?

   A. Ensure that the security group allows Outbound SSH traffic from the IT Administrator's Workstation

   B. Ensure that the security group allows Inbound SSH traffic from the IT Administrator's Workstation

   C. Ensure the Network Access Control Lists allow Outbound SSH traffic from the IT Administrator's Workstation

   D. Ensure the Network Access Control Lists allow Inbound SSH traffic from the IT Administrator's Workstation

69. An organization uses the AWS cloud for creating a private connection from on-premises IT infrastructure to AWS. Now, they want a solution of getting core benefits of traffic encryption, while ensuring that the latency is kept to minimum. How would they achieve their requirement? (choose any 2)

   A. AWS NAT gateways

   B. AWS VPC Peering

   C. AWS Direct Connect

   D. AWS VPN

70. From the following options, which is best to generate encryption keys based on FIPS 140-2 level 3? (choose any 2)

   A. AWS Cloud HSM

   B. AWS KMS

   C. AWS managed keys

   D. AWS Customer Keys

71. A huge multinational enterprise has thousands of EC2 instances on AWS, and now they want to make sure that all servers are not occupying any critical security flaws. How can this requirement be fulfilled? (choose any 2)

   A. Use AWS Config to ensure that the servers have no critical flaws

   B. Use AWS SSM to patch the servers

C. Use AWS Inspector to ensure that the servers have no critical flaws

D. Use AWS Inspector to patch the servers

72. In Amazon Linux AMI instances, a company is trying to use AWS Systems Manager. The command run does not work on a number of instances. How would they diagnose the problem? (choose any 2)

A. Ensure the security groups allow outbound communication for the Instance

B. Ensure the right AMI is used for the Instance

C. Check the /var/log/amazon/ssm/errors.log file

D. Ensure that the SSM agent is running on the target machine

73. A company has an EC2 instance with EBS volume, and encryption of this is done via KMS. Now, some hacker deletes the customer key that is used for encryption. Then how can they decrypt the data?

A. Use AWS Config to recover the key

B. Request AWS Support to recover the key

C. You cannot decrypt the data that was encrypted under the CMK, and the data is not recoverable

D. Create a new Customer Key using KMS and attach it to the existing volume

74. You must use the keys available in the CloudFront to serve private content. How is this possible?

A. Use AWS Access keys

B. Create a pre-signed URL's

C. Add the keys to the S3 bucket

D. Add the keys to the backend distribution

75. For a number of EC2 instances, you must perform penetration tests on the AWS Cloud. How can you do this? (choose any 2)

A. Use an appropriate Penetration testing tool

B. Choose any of the AWS instance types

C. Get prior approval from AWS for conducting the test

D. Work with an AWS partner and no need for prior approval request from AWS

76. The AWS KMS service provides you with a set of customer keys. These keys were used for approximately six months. Now, you are attempting to use new KMS functions for the existing key set, but you are unable to do so. What could be the issue behind this?
   A. You have not explicitly given access via IAM users
   B. You have not given access via the IAM roles
   C. You have not explicitly given access via the IAM policy
   D. You have not explicitly given access via the key policy

77. If you want to use your own DNS managed instance rather than using AWS DNS service for routing DNS request from the instance in VPC then how would you do this?
   A. Change the subnet configuration to allow DNS requests from the new DNS Server
   B. Change the route table for the VPC
   C. Create a new DHCP options set and replace the existing one
   D. Change the existing DHCP options set

78. How do you make sure to inspect the running process on EC2 instance without interrupting its continuous running for security issues?
   A. Use AWS Config to see the changed process information on the server
   B. Use the SSM Run command to send the list of running processes information to an S3bucket
   C. Use AWS CloudWatch to record the processes running on the server
   D. Use AWS Cloudtrail to record the processes running on the server to an S3 bucket

79. A company hired you and assigned you a task to make sure that AWS and its on-site Active Directory are federated authentication mechanisms. What are the important steps that must be taken in this process? (choose any 2)
   A. Configure AWS as the relying party in Active Directory Federation Services
   B. Configure AWS as the relying party in Active Directory
   C. Ensure the right match is in place for On-premise AD Groups and IAM Roles
   D. Ensure the right match is in place for On-premise AD Groups and IAM Groups

80. If you want to get the point in time API activity of any suspicious API activity that occurred 15 days ago. How would you get that?
   A. Use AWS Config to get the API calls which were made 15 days ago

B. Search the Cloud Watch metrics to find for the suspicious activity, which occurred 15 days ago

C. Search the Cloudtrail event history on the API events, which occurred 15 days ago.

D. Search the Cloud Watch logs to find for the suspicious activity, which occurred 15 days ago

81. A set of EC2 instances is currently held by your company in the VPC. The IT Security department suspects that the instances will be attacked by DDos. What can you do to minify the chances of attack on the IP addresses that receive a large number of applications?

A. Use AWS Trusted Advisor to get the IP addresses accessing the EC2 Instances

B. Use AWS Config to get the IP addresses accessing the EC2 Instances

C. Use AWS CloudTrail to get the IP addresses accessing the EC2 Instances

D. Use VPC Flow logs to get the IP addresses accessing the EC2 Instances

82. An incident reaction plan was drafted a few months ago by an IT team of the enterprise. The response plan is regularly implemented. Since its inception, no changes has been made to the response plan. Which of the following is the correct plan statement?

A. The response plan is complete in its entirety

B. The response plan does not cater to new services

C. The response plan is not implemented on a regular basis

D. It places too much emphasis on already implemented security controls

83. There is an S3 bucket currently hosted in an AWS account. It contains information that a partner account needs to access. What is the safest way to access S3 buckets in your account with your partner account? (choose any 3)

A. Provide access keys for your account to the partner account

B. Provide the Account Id to the partner account

C. Provide the ARN for the role to the partner account

D. Ensure the partner uses an external id when making the request

E. Ensure an IAM user is created which can be assumed by the partner account

F. Ensure an IAM role is created which can be assumed by the partner account

84. An organization uses AWS to host its web application for which they create EC2 instance in public subnet. Now, they need to connect an EC2 instance which will host Oracle DB. How would they do all this in a secure way? (choose an 2)

    A. Ensure the database security group allows incoming traffic from 0.0.0.0/0
    B. Place the EC2 Instance with the Oracle database in the same public subnet as the Web server for faster communication.
    C. Create a database security group and ensure the web security group to allow incoming access
    D. Place the EC2 Instance with the Oracle database in a separate private subnet

85. A company uses S3 bucket to store log files. These log files are used for analysis after that, they purge these files. How would they do this configuration in S3 bucket?

    A. Enabling CORS on the S3 bucket
    B. Creating an IAM policy for the S3 bucket
    C. Configuring lifecycle configuration rules on the S3 bucket
    D. Adding a bucket policy on the S3 bucket

86. A windows machine in one VPC needs to join the AD domain in another VPC. VPC Peering has been established. But the domain join is not working. What is the other step that needs to be followed in order to ensure that the AD domain join can work as intended?

    A. Ensure that the AD is placed in a public subnet
    B. Ensure the security groups for the AD hosted subnet has the right rule for relevant subnets
    C. Change the VPC peering connection to a Direct Connect connection
    D. Change the VPC peering connection to a VPN connection

87. How do you ensure that the object in the primary region is available in the secondary region on the failure of the primary region? (choose any 2)

    A. Enable the Bucket ACL and add a condition for { "Null": {"aws:MultiFactorAuthAge": true }}
    B. For the Bucket policy add a condition for { "Null": { "aws:MultiFactorAuthAge":true }}
    C. Enable bucket versioning and enable Master Pays
    D. Enable bucket versioning and also enable CRR

88. You try to patch a set of EC2 systems with the Systems Manager. Some of the systems are not covered by the patch. Which of these can be used to resolve the problem? (choose any 3)

    A. Check the Instance status by using the Health API
    B. Ensure that the agent is running on the Instances
    C. Check to see if the IAM user has the right permissions for EC2
    D. Check to see if the right role has been assigned to the EC2 Instances

89. How can I integrate the AWS IAM with a local LDAP (Lightweight Directory Access Protocol) directory service? What technique can be used?

    A. Use IAM roles to automatically rotate the IAM credentials when LDAP credentials are updated.
    B. Use AWS Security Token Service from an identity broker to issue short-lived AWS credentials.
    C. Use SAML (Security Assertion Markup Language) to enable single sign-on between AWS and LDAP.
    D. Use an IAM policy that references the LDAP account identifiers and the AWS credentials.

90. How do you make CloudTrail logs encrypted when they are being delivered in AWS account?

    A. Enable KMS encryption for the logs which are sent to CloudWatch
    B. Enable S3-KMS for the underlying bucket which receives the log files
    C. Enable S3-SSE for the underlying bucket which receives the log files
    D. Do not do anything since CloudTrail logs are automatically encrypted

91. A company has an application which currently uses customer keys which are generated via AWS KMS in the US East region. Now, they want to use the same set of keys from the EU-Central region. How can this be accomplished?

    A. This is not possible since keys from KMS are region specific
    B. Use the backing key from the US east region and use it in the EU-Central region
    C. Use key rotation and rotate the existing keys to the EU-Central region
    D. Export the key from the US east region and import them into the EU-Central region

92. A set of keys was developed for your company with AWS KMS. You must ensure that only certain services are used for each key. For instance, they want to use only one key for the S3 service. How can you do that?

    A. Define an IAM user , allocate the key and then assign the permissions to the required service
    B. Use the kms:ViaService condition in the Key policy
    C. Create a bucket policy that allows the key to get accessed only by the S3 service
    D. Create an IAM policy that allows the key to being accessed only by the S3 service

93. An enterprise is using AWS to host its java-based application on EC2 instance. That application can access the DynamoDB table and currently instance serving production based user. How securely an instance can access the DynamoDB table?

    A. Use IAM Access Groups with the right permissions to interact with DynamoDB and assign it to the EC2 Instance
    B. Use IAM Access Keys with the right permissions to interact with DynamoDB and assign it to the EC2 Instance
    C. Use KMS keys with the right permissions to interact with DynamoDB and assign it to the EC2 Instance
    D. Use IAM Roles with permissions to interact with DynamoDB and assign it to the EC2 Instance

94. A company uses a cluster Redshift to store its data storage facility. The Internal IT Security team is required to ensure that Redshift database data should be encrypted. How can we accomplish that?

    A. Use S3 Encryption
    B. Use SSL/TLS for encrypting the data
    C. Use AWS KMS Customer Default master key
    D. Encrypt the EBS volumes of the underlying EC2 Instances

95. An enterprise uses S3 to put its critical data and metadata. They want all of their data and metadata to be encrypted. What steps are needed to ensure that metadata is encrypted?

    A. Put the metadata in the S3 bucket itself
    B. Put the metadata in a DynamoDB table and ensure the table is encrypted during creation time

C. Put the metadata as metadata for each object in the S3 bucket and then enable S3 Server KMS encryption

D. Put the metadata as metadata for each object in the S3 bucket and then enable S3 Server-side encryption.

96. A security team must submit daily briefings to the CISO containing a report that misses out on the latest security patches on thousands of EC2 instances and on-site servers. All servers must comply within 24 hours to ensure that they do not appear in the report on the next day. How does the security team meet these requirements?

A. Use a Trusted Advisor to generate the report of out of compliance instances/ servers. Use Systems Manager Patch Manager to install the missing patches

B. Use Systems Manager Patch Manager to generate the report of out of compliance instances/ servers. Redeploy all out of compliance instances/servers using an AMI with the latest patches

C. Use Systems Manager Patch Manager to generate the report of out of compliance instances/ servers. Use Systems Manager Patch Manager to install the missing patches

D. Use Amazon QuickSight and Cloud Trail to generate the report of out of compliance instances/servers. Redeploy all out of compliance instances/servers using an AMI with the latest patches

97. An organization uses a number of EC2 instances and wants to identify the SG that allows unrestricted access to the resource. How would they fulfill their requirement?

A. Use the AWS CLI to query the security groups and then filter for the rules which have unrestricted access

B. Use AWS Config to see which security groups have compromised access

C. Use the AWS Trusted Advisor to see which security groups have compromised access

D. Use AWS Inspector to inspect all the security Groups

98. A company uses AWS KMS service to create customer keys. These keys are used for 6 months and now they are trying to use new KMS features for an existing set of keys but are unable to do that. Why is that?

A. You have not explicitly given access via IAM users

B. You have not given access via the IAM roles

C. You have not explicitly given access via the bucket policy

D. You have not explicitly given access via the key policy

99. For your AWS account, an enterprise has specified privileged users. They are the administrator for key corporate resources. The security authentication for these users is now mandated to improve. How can this be done?

   A. Disable root access for the users
   B. Enable accidental deletion for these user accounts
   C. Enable versioning for these user accounts
   D. Enable MFA for these user accounts

100. From the following options, which is not the best practice of security audit?

   A. Wherever there are changes in your organization, such as people leaving
   B. Conduct an audit if you ever suspect that an unauthorized person might have accessed your account
   C. Conduct an audit if application instances have been added to your account
   D. Conduct an audit on a yearly basis

101. In the event, an employee will be performing unauthorized actions on AWS infrastructure, if he succeeds, a security team will execute a response plan. They want to include steps to see it as part of the incident that the IAM permissions of the employee have changed. Which steps the planning team should document?

   A. Use AWS Config to examine the employee's IAM permissions prior to the incident and compare them to the employee's current IAM permissions
   B. Use a Trusted Advisor to examine the employee's IAM permissions prior to the incident and compare them to the employee's current IAM permissions
   C. Use Macie to examine the employee's IAM permissions prior to the incident and compare them to the employee's current IAM permissions
   D. Use CloudTrail to examine the employee's IAM permissions prior to the incident and compare them to the employee's current IAM permissions

102. In the AWS test environment, you have an instance setup. The required application has been installed, and the server has been promoted into a production environment. You have advised your IT Security team that traffic might flow to port 22 from an unknown IP address. How can we immediately mitigate this?

   A. Change the Instance type for the Instance
   B. Change the AMI for the instance

C. Remove the rule for incoming traffic on port 22 for the Security Group

D. Shutdown the instance

103. A company uses AWS KMS in the us-east region to generate customer keys, and they want to use the same keys in the EU- Central region. How would they do this?

A. This is not possible since keys from KMS are region specific

B. Use the backing key from the US east region and use it in the EU-Central region

C. Use key rotation and rotate the existing keys to the EU-Central region

D. Export the key from the US east region and import them into the EU-Central region

104. An organization wants to use Lambda function to put metadata of objects in the DynamoDB table, whenever the data gets stored in S3. How would they give Lambda function access to DynamoDB table?

A. Create an IAM service role with permissions to write to the DynamoDB table. Associate that role with the Lambda function

B. Create an IAM user with permissions to write to the DynamoDB table. Store an access key for that user in the Lambda environment variables

C. Create a resource policy that grants the Lambda function permissions to write to the DynamoDB table. Attach the policy to the DynamoDB table

D. Create a VPC endpoint for DynamoDB within a VPC. Configure the Lambda function to access resources in the VPC

105. For development purposes, your development team has begun to use AWS resources. It was just created for the AWS account. Your IT safety team is concerned that AWS keys might leak. What is the first level of action to safeguard the AWS account?

A. Restrict access using IAM policies

B. Create IAM Roles

C. Create IAM Groups

D. Delete the AWS keys for the root account

106. A company uses CloudTrail in all of its accounts to log all AWS API operations for all regions. The CISO has called for additional steps to safeguard the integrity of the log files. How many steps will prevent intentional or unintended alteration of the log files? (choose any 2)

A. Create a Security Group that blocks all traffic except calls from the CloudTrail service. Associate the security group with all the Cloud Trail destination S3 buckets

B. Use Systems Manager Configuration Compliance to continually monitor the access policies of S3 buckets containing Cloud Trail Logs

C. Enable Cloud Trail log file integrity validation

D. Write a Lambda function that queries the Trusted Advisor Cloud Trail checks. Run the function every 10 minutes

E. Create an S3 bucket in a dedicated log account and grant other accounts write-only access. Deliver all log files from every account to this S3 bucket

107. For an EC2 instance, you want to receive a list of vulnerabilities according to the directives of the Internet Security Center. What will you do about it?

A. Use AWS Macie

B. Use AWS Inspector

C. Use AWS Trusted Advisor

D. Enable AWS Guard Duty for the Instance

108. An EC2 instance application must use username and password to access a database. These secrets have been saved in the SSM Parameter Store using the default KMS CMK type SecureString. Which configuration step combination will enable the application to access the secrets through API? (choose any 2)

A. Add the SSM service role as a trusted service to the EC2 instance role

B. Add permission to use the KMS key to decrypt to the EC2 instance role

C. Add permission to read the SSM parameter to the EC2 instance role

D. Add permission to use the KMS key to decrypt to the SSM service role

E. Add the EC2 instance role as a trusted service to the SSM service role

109. In various regions, your enterprise has a wide range of accounts, which include resources like EC2, CloudWatch, DynamoDB, EBS, Redshift, RDS, S3, Elastic BeanStalk, IAM, Autoscaling and Elastic Load Balancer. A compliance report of all the resources used by your firm is required by the IT Audit department. Which of these will help you to report as quickly as possible?

A. Use AWS Config to get the list of all resources

B. Use Cloud Trail to get the list of all resources

C. Create a bash shell script with the AWS CLI. Query for all resources in all regions. Store the results in an S3 bucket

D. Create a PowerShell script using the AWS CLI. Query for all resources with the tag of production

110. An enterprise uses VPC to host its application. Inside VPC web and database, tier is hosted. During testing, they observed that the app home page is unreachable even after checking security group. How would they identify the issue?

A. Use AWS Guard Duty to analyze the traffic

B. Use AWS WAF to analyze the traffic

C. Use VPC Flow logs to diagnose the traffic

D. Use the AWS Trusted Advisor to see what can be done

111. An organization needs to perform a penetration test on its AWS resources to analyze the security of the infrastructure. How would they do this?

A. Use a custom AWS Marketplace solution for conducting the penetration test

B. Submit a request to AWS Support

C. Turn on VPC Flow Logs and carry out the penetration test

D. Turn on Cloud trail and carry out the penetration test

112. You have multiple EC2 instances running from the long duration and now you want to identify if there is any Security group which allows unrestricted access to the resource. How would you fulfill this requirement?

A. Use the AWS CLI to query the security groups and then filter for the rules which have unrestricted access

B. Use AWS Config to see which security groups have compromised access

C. Use the AWS Trusted Advisor to see which security groups have compromised access

D. Use AWS Inspector to inspect all the security Groups

113. Which AWS service does an enterprise use to record all AWS KMS service calls?

A. Use CloudWatch metrics

B. Enable CloudWatch logs

C. Enable logging on the KMS service

D. Enable a trail in CloudTrail

114. An organization needs IDS for its VPC in AWS. From the following option which is the best option to implement?

   A. Use a custom solution available in the AWS Marketplace
   B. Use AWS CloudWatch to monitor all traffic
   C. Use VPC Flow logs to detect the issues and flag them accordingly
   D. Use AWS WAF to catch all intrusions occurring on the systems in the VPC

115. Company's AWS administrator provisioned EC2 instance with EBS volumes, having encryption key alias "aws/ebs" as part of code deployment. When will the selected KMS key be rotated?

   A. After 3 years
   B. After 365 days
   C. After 128 days
   D. After 30 days

116. An organization uses Lambda function, which reads metadata from an object called S3 and saves it in a table called DynamoDB. Whenever an object is saved inside the bucket S3, the feature is activated. How doeSSH the Lambda feature access the DynamoDB table?

   A. Create an IAM user with permissions to write to the DynamoDB table. Store an access key for that user in the Lambda environment variables
   B. Create a VPC endpoint for DynamoDB within a VPC. Configure the Lambda function to access resources in the VPC
   C. Create an IAM service role with permissions to write to the DynamoDB table. Associate that role with the Lambda function
   D. Create a resource policy that grants the Lambda function permissions to write to the DynamoDB table. Attach the policy to the DynamoDB table

117. An enterprise uses VPC for subnets, now private subnet of VPC needs access to KMS service. How would they do this?

   A. Use VPC Peering
   B. Attach a VPN connection to the VPC
   C. Attach an Internet gateway to the subnet
   D. Use a VPC endpoint

118. You want a secure way of generating, storing and managing cryptographic keys with exclusive access for the keys. How would you fulfill this requirement?
    A. Use KMS and the normal KMS encryption keys
    B. Use Cloud HSM
    C. Use S3 Server Side Encryption
    D. Use KMS and use an external key material

119. A company uses S3 to host website. It has some web pages that use JavaScript, which can access resources in another bucket on which web site hosting is also enabled. But when users access the web pages, they are getting a blocked JavaScript error. How can you rectify this?
    A. Enable CRR for the bucket
    B. Enable MFA for the bucket
    C. Enable CORS for the bucket
    D. Enable versioning for the bucket

120. How do you encrypt the CloudTrail logs?
    A. Enable Server-side encryption for the destination S3 bucket
    B. Enable Server-side encryption for the trail
    C. There is no need to do anything since the logs will already be encrypted
    D. Enable SSL certificates for the CloudTrail logs

121. An enterprise gets an email that their AWS account has been compromised, then what steps should be taken? (choose any 3)
    A. Change the password for all IAM users
    B. Keep all resources running to avoid disruption
    C. Rotate all IAM access keys
    D. Change the root account password

122. In an AWS testing environment, you have an instance setup. The application has been installed, and the server has been promoted into a production environment. Your IT Security team has informed you that traffic may flow from an unknown IP to port 22. How can this be immediately mitigated? (choose any 2)
    A. Change the AMI for the instance
    B. Shutdown the instance
    C. Change the Instance type for the Instance

D. Remove the rule for incoming traffic on port 22 for the Security Group

123. How do you assign limited access to the user for a specific duration to object in S3 bucket?

    A. Use IAM policies with a timestamp to limit the access
    B. Use IAM Roles with a timestamp to limit the access
    C. Use Pre-signed URL's
    D. Use versioning and enable a timestamp for each version

124. You define the below custom bucket policy

```
{
  "Version":"2012-10-17",
  "Statement":[
    {
      "Sid":"Stmt1234567890123",
      "Effect":"Allow",
      "Principal": "*",
      "Action":["s3:GetObject"],
      "Resource":["arn:aws:s3:::appbucket]
    }
  ]
}
```

When applying this policy, you get an error "action does not apply to any resources in statement". Why?

    A. Create the bucket "appbucket" and then apply the policy
    B. Change the Resource section to "arn:aws:s3:::appbucket/*"
    C. Verify that the policy has the same name as the bucket name. If not, make it the same
    D. Change the IAM permissions by applying for PutBucketPolicy permissions

125. An EC2 instance application must have a username and password to access a database. The Developer saved those secrets in the SSM Parameter Store, using KMS CMK as default and using SecureString type. How do you use the API to access the secrets by combining configuration steps? (choose any 2)

    A. Add the SSM service role as a trusted service to the EC2 instance role
    B. Add permission to use the KMS key to decrypt to the EC2 instance role

C. Add permission to use the KMS key to decrypt to the SSM service role

D. Add permission to read the SSM parameter to the EC2 instance role

E. Add the EC2 instance role as a trusted service to the SSM service role

126. An organization in AWS has multiple resources, and they want to request a get list of resources across the account. How would they do this?

A. Use AWS Config to get the list of all resources

B. Use Cloud Trail to get the list of all resources

C. Create a bash shell script with the AWS CLI. Query for all resources in all regions. Store the results in an S3 bucket

D. Create a power shell script using the AWS CLI. Query for all resources with the tag of production

127. You have an EC2 instance hosted in your company by an AWS VPC. Logs from an EC2 instance must be stored accordingly. There is a requirement; access for the purpose of log files should also be limited. How can this be done? (choose any 2)

A. Create an IAM policy that gives the desired level of access to the CloudWatch Log group

B. Create an IAM policy that gives the desired level of access to the Cloudtrail trail

C. Stream the log files to a separate Cloudtrail trail

D. Stream the log files to a separate CloudWatch Log group

128. Your company needs notification to monitor all root user activity. How can this be done? (choose any 2)

A. Use Cloudtrail API call

B. Use a Lambda function

C. Create a CloudWatch Logs Rule

D. Create a CloudWatch Events Rule

129. An enterprise uses AWS to host its internal network. Now, they need to use the machine inside VPC, which could authenticate private certificates and also minimize work and maintenance in working with certificates. How would they do this?

A. Consider using AWS Trusted Advisor for managing the certificates

B. Consider using AWS Access keys to generate the certificates

C. Consider using AWS Certificate Manager

D. Consider using Windows Server 2016 Certificate Manager

130. An organization uses CloudTrail to log API activities in all regions from all accounts. Now, the CEO wants to follow some steps to protect the integrity of log files. How can they protect log files from intentional and unintentional alteration? (choose any 2)

   A. Create a Security Group that blocks all traffic except calls from the CloudTrail service. Associate the security group with all the Cloud Trail destination S3 buckets

   B. Use Systems Manager Configuration Compliance to continually monitor the access policies of S3 buckets containing Cloud Trail Logs

   C. Write a Lambda function that queries the Trusted Advisor Cloud Trail checks. Run the function every 10 minutes

   D. Enable Cloud Trail log file integrity validation

   E. Create an S3 bucket in a dedicated log account and grant the other accounts write-only access. Deliver all log files from every account to this S3 bucket

131. How does an organization acquire the list of vulnerabilities of EC2 instance as per the requirement of internet security center?

   A. Use AWS Macie

   B. Use AWS Inspector

   C. Use AWS Trusted Advisor

   D. Enable AWS Guard Duty for the Instance

132. An enterprise uses EBS volume for underlying EC2 instance and they want that all the data on the volume must be encrypted. How would they fulfill their requirement?

   A. IAM Access Key

   B. API Gateway with STS

   C. AWS Certificate Manager

   D. AWS KMS API

133. In AWS, you have a 2-tier application. It consists of a separate EC2 Instance web server and database server (SQL Server). These EC2 instances security groups are created by you. The Web level must be accessed through the Internet by users. A web security group(wg-123) and the security database group(db-345) have been created. Which combination of the following rules will enable a safe and functional application? (choose any 2)

   A. db-345- Allow ports 1433 from 0.0.0.0/0

   B. wg-123- Allow port 1433 from wg-123

    C. db-345- Allow port 1433 from wg-123

    D. wg-123- Allow ports 80 and 443 from 0.0.0.0/0

134. An organization has privileged users for AWS account, and these users are the administrators of key resources. So, they want to enhance the security authentication for these users. How would they do this?

    A. Disable root access for the users

    B. Enable accidental deletion for these user accounts

    C. Enable versioning for these user accounts

    D. Enable MFA for these user accounts

135. An organization uses CloudFront behind the website, and now they want their website to be protected from any sort of SQL injection or Cross-site scripting attacks. How would they do this?

    A. AWS Config

    B. AWS Inspector

    C. AWS WAF

    D. AWS Trusted Advisor

136. An enterprise uses HTTPS traffic to allow its users to access the website. They also open port 22 for administrative perspective. The administrative IP is 203.0.113.1/32. What type of SG configuration is needed for most secure but functional support of requirements? (choose any 2)

    A. Port 22 coming from 203.0.113.1/32

    B. Port443 coming from 0.0.0.0/0

    C. Port22 coming from 0.0.0.0/0

    D. Port22 coming from 0.0.0.0/0

137. To provide AWS access to an employee in an organization, an AWS user account is created. You want to limit the access to the resources over a short period with a policy for that user alone. What is the ideal policy to use as follows?

    A. A bucket ACL

    B. A Bucket Policy

    C. An Inline Policy

    D. An AWS Managed Policy

138. A company hosts a common web application that connects to an Amazon RDS MySQL DB instance with default ACL in a private VPC subnet. The department of IT Security is suspected of being attacked by a suspect IP. How does the subnet protect against this attack?

    A. Change the Outbound NACL to deny access from the suspecting IP
    B. Change the Inbound NACL to deny access from the suspecting IP
    C. Change the Outbound Security Groups to deny access from the suspecting IP
    D. Change the Inbound Security Groups to deny access from the suspecting IP

139. A web app operates behind an Application Load Balancer in a VPC on EC2 instances. In an RDS MySQL DB instance, the application saves data. A Linux bastion host is used to update schematic to a database–managers connect from a business workstation to the host, via SSH. The infrastructure is covered by the following security groups
    • sgBastion – associated with the bastion host
    • sgDB – associated with the database
    • sgWeb – associated with the EC2 instances
    • sgLB – associated with the ELB
      From the above SG configuration, which allows the application to be secure and functional?

    A. sgLB: Allows port 80 and 443traffic from 0.0.0.0/0 sgWeb: Allows port 80 and 443 traffic from sgLB sgDB: Allow port 3306 traffic from sgWeb and sgBastion sgBastion: Allows port 22traffic from the corporate IP address range
    B. sgLB: Allows port 80 and 443traffic from 0.0.0.0/0 sgWeb: Allows port 80 and 443 traffic from sgLB sgDB: Allows port 3306 traffic from sgWeb and sgBastion sgBastion: Allows port 22traffic from the VPC IP address range
    C. sgLB: Allows port 80 and 443traffic from 0.0.0.0/0 sgWeb: Allows port 80 and 443 traffic from sgLB sgDB: Allows port 3306 traffic from sgWeb and sgLB sgBastion: Allow port 22traffic from the VPC IP address range
    D. sgLB: Allows port 80 and 443traffic from 0.0.0.0/0 sgWeb: Allows port 80 and 443 traffic from 0.0.0.0/0 sgDB: Allows port 3306 traffic from sgWeb and sgBastion sgBastion: Allows port 22traffic from the corporate IP address range

140. A company would like to enable Single Sign-On (SSO) to allow its employees with their corporate directory identity to access the management console. What steps are needed in the process from below? (choose any 2)

A. Create an IAM role that establishes a trust relationship between IAM and the corporate directory identity provider (IdP)

B. Create a Direct Connect connection between on-premise network and AWS. Use an AD connector for connecting AWS with on-premise active directory

C. Create IAM users that can be mapped to the employees' corporate identities

D. Create a Lambda function to assign IAM roles to the temporary security tokens provided to the users

E. Create IAM policies that can be mapped to group memberships in the corporate directory

141. How does an enterprise assign right level of permission to a user, developers and IT team on API gateway?

A. Use IAM Access Keys to create sets of keys for the different types of users

B. Use the AWS Config tool to manage the permissions for the different users

C. Use IAM Policies to create different policies for the different types of users

D. Use the secure token service to manage the permissions for the different users

142. An enterprise is looking for a solution to avoid traversing of data over the internet. The data of application will traverse to and from the S3 bucket. The application is running on EC2 instances in a private subnet. How would they find a solution?

A. Access the S3 bucket through the SSL protected S3 endpoint

B. Access the S3 bucket through a VPC endpoint for S3

C. Access the S3 bucket through a NAT gateway

D. Access the S3 bucket through a proxy server

143. An organization has its external vendors who deliver the files to the organization. These vendors are cross-accounted and provided permissions to upload objects to one of the S3 buckets of the organization. What combination of steps must the seller take to allow the user to access the uploaded files? (choose any 2)

A. Upload the file to the company's S3 bucket

B. Add a bucket policy to the bucket that grants the bucket owner full permission to the object

C. Encrypt the object with a KMS key controlled by the company

D. Add a grant to the object's ACL giving full permissions to bucket owner

E. Attach an IAM role to the bucket that grants the bucket owner full permission to the object

144. You create an extensive, confidential web documentation server on AWS, which is stored in all documentation on S3. One of the requirements is that it should not be accessed directly from S3 to the public and that you must use CloudFront. Which of the following methods would satisfy the outlined requirements?

A. Create an S3 bucket policy that lists the CloudFront distribution ID as the Principal and the target bucket as the Amazon Resource Name (ARN)

B. Create individual policies for each bucket in which the documents are stored and in that policy grant access to only CloudFront

C. Create an Origin Access Identity (OAI) for CloudFront and grant access to the objects in your S3 bucket to that OAI

D. Create an Identity and Access Management (IAM)user for CloudFront and grant access to the objects in your S3 bucket to that IAM User

145. How does an enterprise automate the administrative tasks on EC2 instances in AWS account?

A. Use AWS Config

B. Use the AWS Inspector

C. Use the AWS Systems Manager Run Command

D. Use the AWS Systems Manager Parameter Store

146. A new web-based application is being deployed on AWS. They are expected to be the target of frequent DDoS attacks based on their other web applications. What steps can the company take to safeguard its application? (choose any 2)

A. Enable GuardDuty to block malicious traffic from reaching the application

B. Use CloudFront and AWS WAF to prevent malicious traffic from reaching the application

C. Use Amazon Inspector on the EC2 instances to examine incoming traffic and discard malicious traffic

D. Use an ELB Application Load Balancer and Auto Scaling group to scale to absorb application layer traffic

E. Associate the EC2 instances with a security group that blocks traffic from blacklisted IP addresses

147. An enterprise has a legacy application that displays all logs in a local text file. Logs from all AWS-operated applications need to be monitored continuously for safety-

related messages. What can the company do to deploy the legacy Amazon EC2 application, and to comply with the surveillance requirement?

A. Export the local text log files to CloudTrail. Create a Lambda function that queries the CloudTrail logs for security incidents using Athena

B. Install the Amazon Inspector agent on any EC2 instance running the legacy application. Generate CloudWatch alerts based on any Amazon Inspector findings

C. Send the local text log files to CloudWatch Logs and configure a CloudWatch metric filter. Trigger CloudWatch alarms based on the metrics

D. Create a Lambda function that mounts the EBS volume with the logs and scans the logs for security incidents. Trigger the function every 5 minutes with a scheduled CloudWatch event

148. How does an organization encrypt the data stored in AWS at rest? (choose any 2)

A. When storing data in S3, enable server-side encryption

B. When storing data in Amazon EC2 Instance Store, encrypt the volume by using KMS

C. When storing data in Amazon S3, use object versioning and MFA Delete

D. When storing data in EBS, encrypt the volume by using AWS KMS

E. When storing data in Amazon EBS, use only EBS–optimized Amazon EC2 instances

149. From the following option, which is a secure way of accessing EC2 Linux instance?

A. AWS SDK keys

B. AWS Access keys

C. Key pairs

D. IAM User name and password

150. Organization policy requires the disability on all servers of any unsafe server protocols, such as FTP, Telnet, HTTP, etc. With a planned CloudWatch event, the security team would like to check all servers regularly to ensure that the current infrastructure is complied with the policies. Which process from the following options will check the compliance of instances?

A. Run an Amazon Inspector assessment using the Runtime Behavior Analysis rules package against every EC2 instance

B. Enable a GuardDuty threat detection analysis targeting the port configuration on every EC2 instance

C. Query the Trusted Advisor API for all best practice security checks and check for "action recommended" status

D. Trigger an AWS Config Rules evaluation of the restricted-common-ports rule against every EC2 instance

151. An enterprise wants to deploy an application on AWS, which can meet the PCI compliance for its control set. They also want to monitor the logs of the web application to identify malicious activity. How would they meet their requirement? (choose any 2)

A. Amazon Cloudtrail

B. Amazon CloudWatch Logs

C. Amazon VPC Flow Logs

D. Amazon AWS Config

152. An enterprise uses S3 to store its secret data and want that available on S3 in multiple geographical locations. How do you, as an architect, provide a solution for this requirement?

A. Enable Cross region replication for the S3 bucket

B. Create a snapshot of the S3 bucket and copy it to another region

C. Copy the data to an EBS Volume in another Region

D. Apply Multi-AZ for the underlying S3 bucket

153. An enterprise has multiple CMKs, that have imported key material. From the following options, which is best to choose for the key rotation? (choose any 2)

A. Delete an existing CMK, and a new default CMK will be created

B. Import new key material to a new CMK; point the key alias to the new CMK

C. Enable Automatic Key rotation for a CMKs that have imported key material

D. Import new key material to an existing CMK

E. Use CLI or console to explicitly rotate CMKs that have imported key material

154. An organization will ensure for deviation from compliance rules, that any infrastructure launched in the AWS account should be monitored, in particular, that all EC2 instances are launched from a specified list of AMIs and all the attached EBS volumes be encrypted. The non-compliant infrastructure should be stopped. From the following options, which is the best to meet this requirement? (choose any 2)

A. Trigger a CLI command from a CloudWatch event that terminates the infrastructure
B. Monitor compliance with AWS Config Rules triggered by configuration changes
C. Trigger a Lambda function from CloudWatch event of event type "Compliance Rules Notification Change" that terminates the non-compliant infrastructure
D. Set up a CloudWatch event based on Amazon inspector findings
E. Set up a CloudWatch event based on Trusted Advisor metrics

155. A company has a set of keys that uses KMS service and now, they want to stop some keys but they do not know which service is using those keys. So, how will they safely stop using the keys?

A. Change the key material for the key
B. Set an alias for the key
C. Disable the keys
D. Delete the keys since there is a 7 -day waiting period before deletion

156. An enterprise uses AWS for its infrastructure, and now they want to monitor all API calls and also store them for future purpose. But the logs that are older than 6 months must be archived. How would they fulfill their requirement? (Choose any 2)

A. Ensure a lifecycle policy, which is defined on the S3 bucket to move the data to Amazon Glacier after 6 months
B. Enable CloudTrail logging in all accounts into S3 buckets
C. Ensure a lifecycle policy is defined on the S3 bucket to move the data to EBS volumes after 6 months
D. Enable CloudTrail logging in all accounts into Amazon Glacier

157. An application running on EC2 instances in a VPC needs TLS (port 443) to call an external web service. The instances take place in public subnets. Which of the settings mentioned below will allow the application to operate and minimize instance exposure? (choose any 2)

A. A security group with rules that allow outgoing traffic on port 443 and incoming traffic on port 443
B. A security group with rules that allow outgoing traffic on port 443 and incoming traffic on ephemeral ports
C. A security group with a rule that allows outgoing traffic on port 443

D. A network ACL with rules that allow outgoing traffic on port 443 and incoming traffic on port 443

E. A network ACL with rules that allow outgoing traffic on port 443 and incoming traffic on ephemeral ports

F. A network ACL with a rule that allows outgoing traffic on port 443

158. A company wants to check active EBS volumes, snapshots and Elastic IP address, in order to identify that it does not go beyond the service limit. How would they fulfill this requirement?

A. AWS SNS

B. AWS Trusted Advisor

C. AWS EC2

D. AWS CloudWatch

159. When there is VPC peering between two VPC's on which a set of application is running, but applications are still unable to communicate over the peering connection. What kind of troubleshooting is needed to mitigate the issue?

A. Check the Route tables for the VPC's

B. Check to see if the VPC has a NAT gateway attached

C. Check to see if the VPC has an Internet gateway attached

D. Check to see if the VPC has an Internet gateway attached

160. To carry out a security audit which of the following options is not a best practice?

A. Whenever there are changes in your organization

B. Conduct an audit if you ever suspect that an unauthorized person might have accessed your account

C. Conduct an audit, if you have added or removed software in your accounts

D. Conduct an audit on a yearly basis

161. A company generates sensitive records continuously, which are stored in an S3 bucket. The SSE - KMS is used for encrypting all of the objects in the bucket with one of the CMKs. Company compliance policies require the encryption of data by the same encryption key for not more than one month. How would they fulfill their requirement?

A. Trigger a Lambda function with a monthly CloudWatch event that rotates the key material in the CMK

B. Trigger a Lambda function with a monthly CloudWatch event that creates a new CMK, updates the S3 bucket to use the new CMK, and deletes the old CMK

C. Trigger a Lambda function with a monthly CloudWatch event that creates a new CMK and updates the S3 bucket to use the new CMK

D. Configure the CMK to rotate the key material every month

162. How do you control the access to S3 buckets when your data is hosted in the bucket? (choose any 2)

A. Use AWS Access Keys

B. Use IAM user policies

C. Use Bucket policies

D. Use the Secure Token service

163. A company has a current setup in AWS with 2 public subnets, one of them with internet-access web servers and the other of the database server's subnet. What changes would add a better security limit to the resources hosted in architecture?

A. Consider creating a private subnet and adding a NAT instance to that subnet

B. Consider moving both the web and database server to a private subnet

C. Consider moving the database server to a private subnet

D. Consider moving the web server to a private subnet

164. An EC2 instance in a VPC has an application, which must access sensitive data in the data center. Access must be encrypted in transit and latency should consistently be low. How will these requirements be fulfilled?

A. A DirectConnect connection between the VPC and data center

B. A VPN between the VPC and the data center

C. A VPN between the VPC and the data center over a DirectConnect connection

D. Expose the data with a public HTTPS endpoint

165. An organization uses S3 bucket to store data, and as per their policy, all services should have logging enabled. How will you assure that logging is enabled when S3 buckets are created in AWS?

A. Use AWS CloudWatch logs to check whether logging is enabled for buckets

B. Use AWS CloudWatch metrics to check whether logging is enabled for buckets

C. Use AWS Config Rules to check whether logging is enabled for buckets

D. Use AWS Inspector to inspect all S3 buckets and enable logging for those where it is not enabled

166. How can you launch your EC2 instance with your own key pair in AWS? (choose any 3)
    A. Import the private key into EC2
    B. Import the public key into EC2
    C. Create a new key pair using the AWS CLI
    D. Use a third party tool to create the Keypair

167. You work in the media industry and have created a web application, where the client can upload photos to your website. In order to be able to work, this Web application must be able to call the S3 API. When maintaining a maximum level of security, where should you store your API credentials?
    A. Pass API credentials to the instance using instance user data
    B. Save your API credentials in a public Github repository
    C. Do not save your API credentials. Instead, create a role in IAM and assign this role to an EC2 instance when you first create it
    D. Save the API credentials to your PHP files

168. A company has a separate account for development and production department, and now they want to take some security preventives; root user and all IAM users in production account should be restricted to access the unneeded services. How would they do this?
    A. Create an IAM policy that denies access to the services. Create a Config Rule that checks that all users have the policy assigned. Trigger a Lambda function that adds the policy when finding missing users
    B. Create an IAM policy that denies access to the services. Associate the policy with an IAM group and enlist all users and the root users in this group
    C. Create a Service Control Policy that denies access to the services. Apply the policy to the root account
    D. Create a Service Control Policy that denies access to the services. Assemble all production accounts in an organizational unit. Apply the policy to that organizational unit

169. A company is hosting a critical AWS Cloud web application. This is a key application to generate revenue for the company. The IT Security team is concerned about possible website attacks by DDos. The senior management also stated that immediate measures should be taken for a possible attack by DDos. In this respect, what should be done?

    A. Consider using CloudWatch logs to monitor traffic for DDoS attack and quickly take actions on a trigger of a potential attack

    B. Consider using the AWS Shield Advanced Service

    C. Consider using VPC Flow logs to monitor traffic for DDoS attack and quickly take actions on a trigger of a potential attack

    D. Consider using the AWS Shield Service

170. A company has an AWS account, and now they are worried about the leakage of AWS keys. How would they prevent this and protect the AWS account?

    A. Restrict access using IAM policies

    B. Create IAM Roles

    C. Create IAM Groups

    D. Delete the AWS keys for the root account

171. A corporation has multiple AWS accounts. They temporarily want to ensure that users from a production-based account can access a staging account. Which of the subsequent is the right way to make sure this access is put in place?

    A. Create an IAM user with Access keys and the right access policies in the staging account

    B. Copy the IAM user from the production-based account to the staging account

    C. Create a Cross Account IAM Role which can be assumed

    D. Create an IAM Group with Access keys and the right access policies in the staging account

172. Your IT Security Administrator has defined the following policy. What does the following policy define?

    A. Allow access to all AWS resources from workstations in the IP range of 152.0.2.0/24

    B. Allow access to all AWS resources from the workstation with an IP of 152.0.2.0

    C. Allow access to all AWS resources except from workstations in the IP range of 152.0.2.0/24

    D. Allow access to all AWS resources except from workstation with an IP of 152.0.2.0

173. Your enterprise has simply started using an AWS account. They want to make sure that they apply the right security principles to the root user for their AWS Account. Which of the following are the proper safety features to put in place? (Choose 2)

A. Ensure that the root account is used for privileged account activities

B. Delete any Access keys which are present for the root account

C. Have a rotation policy in place for changing the root account password

D. Create Access keys and provide them to the respective IT Administrators

174. A development team has developed an application using Access Keys. The application wishes to make requests to a DynamoDB table. The software now needs to be deployed on an EC2 instance. Which of the following is the right way to make sure that the application can access the DynamoDB table?

A. Add the Access Keys in the environment variables on the EC2 Instance

B. Insert the Access Keys in the application as a security measure

C. Create an IAM Role with right permissions and add it to the EC2 Instance

D. Create an IAM User with right permissions and add it to the EC2 Instance

175. An enterprise has a string of AWS accounts and numerous IAM users are defined in every account. For auditing purposes, they need to ensure that all calls to AWS IAM are logged. How can they obtain this?

A. Use the AWS Config service

B. Use the AWS Inspector service

C. Use the AWS CloudWatch service

D. Use the AWS CloudTrail service

176. Multiple IAM users are set up by an organization. The organization wants each IAM user only within the organization and not from outside to access the IAM console. How can that be achieved?

A. Configure the EC2 instance security group, which allows traffic only from the organization's IP range

B. Create an IAM policy with VPC and allow a secure gateway between the organization and AWS Console

C. Create an IAM policy with a condition, which denies access when the IP address range is not from the organization

D. Create an IAM policy with the security group and use that security group for AWS console login

177. What is the result of the following bucket policy?

{
"Statement":[
{
"Sid":"Sid1",
"Action":"s3:*",
"Effect":"Allow",
"Resource":"arn:aws:s3:::mybucket/*.",
"Principal":{
{"AWS":["arn:aws:iam::111111111:user/mark"]}
}
},
{
"Sid":"Sid2",
"Action":"s3:*",
"Effect":"Deny",
"Resource":"arn:aws:s3:::mybucket/*.",
"Principal":{
{"AWS":[
"*"

]
}
}
]
}

Choose the correct option

A. It will allow the user mark from AWS account number 111111111 all access to the bucket but deny everyone else all access to the bucket
B. It will deny all access to the bucket mybucket
C. It will allow all access to the bucket mybucket
D. None of these

178. You have an Amazon VPC with a private subnet and a public subnet that contains a NAT server. By downloading a bootstrapping script from S3, which deploys an

application through the GIT, you have created a group of EC2 instances that configure themselves at start - up.

Which of the following configurations would give us maximum safety?

A. EC2 instances in our private subnet, no EIPs, route outgoing traffic via the NAT

B. EC2 instance in our private subnet, assigned EIPs, and route our outgoing traffic via our IGW

C. EC2 instances in our public subnet, assigned EIPs, and route outgoing traffic via the NAT

D. EC2 instances in our public subnet, no EIPs, route outgoing traffic via the IGW

179. You have many AWS accounts defined in your company and they are all administered through AWS organizations. An S3 bucket with critical data is in one AWS account. What can we do to ensure access to this bucket for all AWS organization users?

A. Ensure the bucket policy has a condition, which involves aws:AccountNumber

B. Ensure the bucket policy has a condition, which involves aws:OrgID

C. Ensure the bucket policy has a condition, which involves aws:PrincipalID

D. Ensure the bucket policy has a condition, which involves aws:PrincipalOrgID

180. EC2 instances on the AWS Cloud were created by a company. All IP addresses accessing the EC2 Instances must be displayed. Which service can contribute to this?

A. Use Security Groups

B. Use AWS VPC Flow Logs

C. Use the AWS Inspector service

D. Use Network ACL's

181. You create a large - scale confidential AWS web documentation server and all the documents are stored on S3. One of the requirements is that it cannot be accessed directly from S3, and CloudFront is needed to do this. Which of the methods listed below would satisfy these requirements?

A. Create an Origin Access Identity (OAI) for CloudFront and grant access to the objects in your S3 bucket to that OAI

B. Create an S3 bucket policy that lists the CloudFront distribution ID as the Principal and the target bucket as the Amazon Resource Name (ARN)

C. Create an Identity and Access Management (IAM) user for CloudFront and grant access to the objects in your S3 bucket to that IAM User

D. Create individual policies for each bucket the documents are stored in and in that policy grant access to only CloudFront

182. A company wants to use an AWS Cloud - based third - party SaaS application. To discover Amazon EC2 resources running within the company's account, the SaaS application needs access to issue several API commands. The company has internal security policies that requires any external access to its environment must comply with the least privilege principles and controls must be in place to ensure that the credentials used by the SaaS vendor cannot be used by any other third party. Which of the following would meet all of these conditions?

   A. Create an IAM user within the enterprise account, assign a user policy to the IAM user that allows only the actions required by the SaaS application. Create a new access and secret key for the user and provide these credentials to the SaaS provider

   B. Create an IAM role for EC2 instances, assign it a policy that allows only the actions required for the SaaS application to work, provide the role ARN to the SaaS provider to use when launching their application instances

   C. Create an IAM role for cross-account access, allow the SaaS provider's account to assume the role and assign it a policy that allows only the actions required by the SaaS application

   D. From the AWS Management Console, navigate to the Security Credentials page and retrieve the access and secret key for your account

183. A company requires that large amounts of data should be transferred between AWS and an on - site location. AWS has an additional requirement for low latency and high traffic consistency. How would you design a hybrid architecture in view of these requirements?

   A. Create a VPN tunnel for private connectivity, which increases network consistency and reduces latency

   B. Create an IPSec tunnel for private connectivity, which increases network consistency and reduces latency

   C. Create a VPC peering connection between AWS and the Customer gateway

   D. Provision a Direct Connect connection to an AWS region using a Direct Connect partner

184. Your company plans to use bastion hosts to manage AWS servers. Which of the following is the best description from a security point of view of a bastion host?

    A. A Bastion host is deployed into an internal subnet and is used to connect to private network resources and is considered as a critical strong point of the network

    B. Bastion hosts allow users to log in using RDP or SSH and use that session to SSH into internal network to access private subnet resources

    C. A Bastion host should maintain extremely tight security and monitoring as it is available to the public

    D. A Bastion host should be on a private subnet and never a public subnet due to security concerns

185. Your development team uses access keys to develop a S3 and DynamoDB access application. A new security policy says that the credentials should not exceed 2 months of age and should be rotated. How can this be achieved?

    A. Delete the user associated with the keys after every 2 months. Then create the user again

    B. Delete the IAM Role associated with the keys after every 2 months. Then create the IAM Role again

    C. Use a script to query the creation date of the keys. If older than 2 months, create new access key and update all applications to use it, inactivate the old key and delete it

    D. Use the application to rotate the keys in every 2 months via the SDK

186. You plan to use the AWS KMS service to manage your application's keys. Which of the following KMS CMK keys can be used for encrypting? (Choose 2 answers)

    A. Large files

    B. Passwords

    C. RSA keys

    D. Image Objects

187. For the past two years, your company has used AWS. They have separate S3 buckets to log the different AWS services. You hired a third - party provider to analyze your log files. They have an AWS account of their own. How do you ensure that the partner account gets access to the log files for analysis on the company's account? (Choose 2 answers)

A. Ensure the IAM user has access for read-only to the S3 buckets
B. Ensure the IAM Role has access for read-only to the S3 buckets
C. Create an IAM user in the company account
D. Create an IAM Role in the company account

188. Select 2 services that can be integrated with the AWS Web application firewall service.
    A. AWS CloudFront
    B. AWS Application Load Balancer
    C. AWS Classic Load Balancer
    D. AWS Lambda

189. A user has enabled versioning on an S3 bucket. For data at rest, the user uses server side encryption. Which statement of the following will apply if the user supplies his own SSE - C encryption keys?
    A. It is possible to have different encryption keys for different versions of the same object
    B. AWS S3 does not allow the user to upload his own keys for server side encryption
    C. The user should use the same encryption key for all versions of the same object
    D. The SSE-C does not work when versioning is enabled

190. An organization launches 2 instances for production and 3 instances for testing. The organization wants a specific group of IAM users to access only the test instances, not the production ones. How can the organization set such policy?
    A. Create an IAM policy with a condition, which allows access to only small instances
    B. Launch the test and production instances in separate regions and allow region wise access to the group
    C. Define the tags on the test and production servers and add a condition to the IAM policy, which allows access to specific tags
    D. Define the IAM policy, which allows access based on the instance ID'

191. A user creates a Lambda function that a CloudWatch Event would trigger. He needs to store the data from these events in a DynamoDB table. How can the user give access to the DynamoDB table for the Lambda function?
    A. Use the AWS Access keys, which has access to DynamoDB and then place it in an S3 bucket

B. Create a VPC endpoint for the DynamoDB table. Access the VPC end point from the Lambda function

C. Put the AWS Access keys in the Lambda function since the Lambda function by default is secure

D. Use an IAM role, which has permissions to the DynamoDB table and attach it to the Lambda function

192. A company plans to use its web application with AWS EC2 and the AWS Cloudfront. Which of the attacks mentioned below are best suited for using Cloudfront?

A. Malware attacks

B. DDoS attacks

C. SQL injection

D. Cross side scripting

193. You have some developers in your LAMP application who say that they want to access your logs. Since you use an AWS Auto Scaling Group, constant recreation of your instances occurs. What would you do to make sure that these developers can access these log files?

A. Setup a central logging server that you can use to archive your logs; archive these logs to an S3 bucket for developer-access

B. Give only the necessary access to the Apache servers so that the developers can gain access to the log files

C. Give root access to your Apache servers to the developers

D. Give read-only access to your developers to the Apache servers

194. Your company is preparing a safety evaluation of AWS use. Which three best IAM practices should be implemented in preparation for this evaluation?

A. Assign IAM users and groups configured with policies granting full privilege access

B. Create individual IAM users

C. Ensure all users have been assigned and are frequently rotating a password, accessID/secret key, and X.509 certificate

D. Configure MFA on the root account and for privileged IAM users

195. AWS account contains a set of 100 EC2 instances. All of these instances must be patched and maintained; each of these instances are in a private subnet. How can you do that? (Choose 2 answers)

A. Ensure that an Internet gateway is present to download the updates
B. Ensure that a NAT gateway is present to download the updates
C. Use the AWS Inspector to patch the updates
D. Use the Systems Manager to patch the instances

196. You have an S3 bucket defined in AWS. Before sending it across the wire, you want to make sure that you encrypt the data. Which of the following options is best for this purpose?
    A. Use a Lambda function to encrypt the data before sending it to the S3 bucket
    B. Enable server side encryption for the S3 bucket. This request will ensure that the data is encrypted first
    C. Enable client side encryption for the S3 bucket
    D. Use the AWS Encryption CLI to encrypt the data first

197. The AWS account of a company is comprised of about 300 IAM users. Now, there is a mandate for 100 IAM users to change access for unlimited privileges to S3. How can you implement this effectively as a system administrator, so that the policy does not need to be applied at the individual user level?
    A. Create an S3 bucket policy with unlimited access, which includes each user's AWS account ID
    B. Create a policy and apply it to multiple users using a JSON script
    C. Use the IAM groups and add users, based upon their role, to different groups and apply the policy to group
    D. Create a new role and add each user to the IAM role

198. You are working with a company that uses AWS resources. One of the key security policies is to ensure that every data is encrypted, both at rest and in transit. Choose the best option for this.
    A. SSL termination on the ELB
    B. Use S3 SSE and use SSL for data in transit
    C. Enabling sticky sessions on your load balancer
    D. Enabling Proxy Protocol

199. For their web and data base applications, your company has been using AWS to host EC2 Instances. You want to have the following compliance check

- Whether any ports other than admin ports such as SSH and RDP are left open
- Whether any ports to the database server other than ones from the web server security group are open

Which of the following can make this easier so that additional configuration changes do not need to be made?

A. AWS Trusted Advisor
B. AWS Inspector
C. AWS GuardDuty
D. AWS Config

200. An organization hosts critical data in S3 bucket. Although the bucket is authorized to do so, they are still concerned about the deletion of the data. How can the risk of deletion of data on the bucket be restricted? (Choose 2 answers)

A. Enable data encryption at rest for the objects in the bucket
B. Enable MFA Delete in the bucket policy
C. Enable versioning on the S3 bucket
D. Enable data in transit for the objects in the bucket

201. You plan to use AWS Config to review your AWS account's resource configuration. You plan to use an existing IAM role for the resources of AWS Config. What is required to ensure that the AWS configuration service works as required?

A. Ensure that there is a grant policy in place for the AWS Config service within the role
B. Ensure that there is a group policy in place for the AWS Config service within the role
C. Ensure that there is a trust policy in place for the AWS Config service within the role
D. Ensure that there is a user policy in place for the AWS Config service within the role

202. Your firm plans to host its AWS resources on AWS. There is a company policy that requires all key pairs to be fully managed in the company. Choose the correct measures to follow this policy.

A. Generating the key pairs for the EC2 Instances using puttygen
B. Using the AWS KMS service for creation of the keys and the company managing the key lifecycle thereafter

C. Use S3 server-side encryption

D. Use the EC2 Key pairs that come with AWS

203. In a private subnet there are a set of Ec2 instances. For applications on these EC2 instances, DynamoDB table access is required. Ensure that traffic should not get carried to the Internet. How is it possible to do so?

A. Use a VPC Peering connection to the DynamoDB table

B. Use a VPC gateway from the VPC

C. Use a VPN connection from the VPC

D. Use a VPC endpoint to the DynamoDB table

204. You plan to develop an AWS application for your company. It is an application based on the web. Users will be authenticated with their Facebook or Google identities. Which step would you take in your web application implementation?

A. Ensure the Security Groups in the VPC only allow requests from the Google and Facebook Authentication servers.

B. Create an OIDC provider in both Google and Facebook

C. Create a SAML provider in AWS

D. Create an OIDC identity provider in AWS

205. A number of AWS S3 buckets have been defined by your company. You should monitor the S3 buckets and find out the IP address of the source and the person who requests a S3 bucket. How can you accomplish that?

A. Monitor the S3 API calls by using CloudWatch logging

B. Enable AWS Inspector for the S3 bucket

C. Monitor the S3 API calls by using CloudTrail logging

D. Enable VPC flow logs to know the source IP addresses

206. The following security configuration applies to an EC2 instance:
    - ICMP inbound allowed on Security Group
    - ICMP outbound not configured on Security Group
    - ICMP inbound allowed on Network ACL
    - ICMP outbound denied on Network ACL

    Which of the following flow records is saved if Flow logs is activated for the instance?

A. A REJECT record for the response based on the NACL

B. A REJECT record for the response based on the Security Group

C. An ACCEPT record for the request based on the NACL

D. An ACCEPT record for the request based on the Security Group

207. A set of EC2 Instances in AWS is defined by your company. Strict security groups are attached to these Ec2 instances. You need to ensure that changes are noted and implemented in the security groups. How can you do that?

A. Use CloudWatch metrics to monitor the activity on the Security Groups. Use filters to search for the changes and use SNS for the notification

B. Use CloudWatch events to be triggered for any changes to the Security Groups. Configure the Lambda function for email notification as well

C. Use CloudWatch logs to monitor the activity on the Security Groups. Use filters to search for the changes and use SNS for the notification

D. Use AWS Inspector to monitor the activity on the Security Groups. Use filters to search for the changes and use SNS for the notification

208. You have to develop a policy and apply it to a single user. How can you do that in the right way?

A. Add an IAM role for the user

B. Add an AWS managed policy for the user

C. Add an inline policy for the user

D. Add a service policy for the user

209. Multiple applications are currently hosting in a VPC. It was noticed, during the monitoring process, that a certain IP address block provides multiple port scans. The internal security team has requested that all offending IP Addresses should be denied for the next 24 hours. Which of the following is the best way to deny access from the specified IP Address, quickly and temporarily?

A. Modify the Windows Firewall settings on all AMI's that your organization uses in that VPC to deny access from the IP address block

B. Add a rule to all of the VPC Security Groups to deny access from the IP Address block

C. Modify the Network ACLs, associated with all public subnets in the VPC to deny access from the IP Address block

D. Create an AD policy to modify the Windows Firewall settings on all hosts in the VPC to deny access from the IP Address block.

210. An organization wants to log all API activities by using CloudTrail. The logging of data events and management events must be separated. How can they do that? (Choose 2 answers)

    A. Create another trail that logs management events to another S3 bucket
    B. Create one trail that logs data events to an S3 bucket
    C. Create another CloudTrail log group for management events
    D. Create one CloudTrail log group for data events

211. The EC2 instance is hosted in AWS by your company. An application is hosted in this EC2 Instance. There are currently a number of problems with this application. You have to check the network packets to see the type of error. Which steps below could help in resolving this problem?

    A. Use another instance. Setup a port to "promiscuous mode" and sniff the traffic to analyze the packets
    B. Use CloudWatch metric
    C. Use a network monitoring tool provided by an AWS partner.
    D. Use the VPC Flow Logs

212. Using the VPC wizard, a user has created a VPC with private and public subnets. The VPC has CIDR 20.0.0.0/16; CIDR 20.0.1.0/24 is used by the public subnet. The user intends to host the public subnet Web Server with port 80 and the private subnet with port 3306, with a database server. A public subnet (WebSecGrp) and private subnet (DBSecGrp) security group is set up by the utiliser. Which of the below mentioned entries is required in the private subnet database security group DBSecGrp?

    A. Allow Outbound on port 3306 for Destination Web Server Security Group WebSecGrp
    B. Allow Outbound on port 80 for Destination NAT Instance IP
    C. Allow Inbound on port 3306 from source 20.0.0.0/16
    D. Allow Inbound on port 3306 for Source Web Server Security Group WebSecGrp

213. Your IT Security team identified a number of vulnerabilities in the company's AWS account across critical EC2 instances. What would be the easiest way to remedy these vulnerabilities?

    A. Use AWS Systems Manager to patch the servers
    B. Use AWS Inspector to patch the servers

C. Use AWS CLI commands to download the updates and patch the servers

D. Create AWS Lambda functions to download the updates and patch the servers

214. A company needs to create a table for DynamoDB. The software architect of the company provided the following DynamoDB table CLI command

aws dynamodb create-table \
--table-name Customers \
--attribute-definitions \
AttributeName=ID,AttributeType=S \
AttributeName=Name,AttributeType=S \
--key-schema \
AttributeName=ID,KeyType=HASH \
AttributeName=Name,KeyType=RANGE \
--provisioned-throughput \
ReadCapacityUnits=10,WriteCapacityUnits=5 \
--sse-specification Enabled=true

Which of the following has been taken care of from a security perspective from the above command?

A. The above command ensures data encryption in transit for the Customer table

B. The right throughput has been specified from a security perspective

C. The above command ensures data encryption at rest for the Customer table

D. Since the ID is hashed, it ensures security of the underlying table

215. The EC2 Instances in AWS are hosted by your company. You want to know if port scans are performed on your AWS EC2 instances. In this respect, which of the following option can help?

A. Use AWS Config to notify of any malicious port scans

B. Use AWS Guard Duty to monitor any malicious port scans

C. Use AWS Inspector to consciously inspect the instances for port scans

D. Use AWS Trusted Advisor to notify of any malicious port scans

216. Your company plans to develop an AWS application. It is an application based on the web. For authentication, the application users use their Facebook or Google identity.

You want the ability to manage user profiles without the need to add additional coding. Select the appropriate option.

A. Use IAM users to manage the user profiles
B. Create a SAML provider in AWS
C. Use AWS Cognito to manage the user profiles
D. Create an OIDC identity provider in AWS

217. A company is hosting sensitive data in an AWS S3 bucket. You must ensure that the bucket is always privately owned. How can this be continuously ensured? (Choose 2 answers)

A. Use AWS Lambda function to change the bucket policy
B. Use AWS Lambda function to change the bucket ACL
C. Use AWS Trusted Advisor API to monitor the changes to the AWS Bucket
D. Use AWS Config to monitor changes to the AWS Bucket

218. In the AWS region of the us-east, you are running a web application. The application runs on an EC2 auto-scaled layer and an RDS Multi - AZ database. You have been asked by your IT security officer to develop a reliable and lasting logging solution for monitoring changes in the EC2, IAM and RDS resources. The solution must ensure that your log data be integral and confidential. Which of these solutions would you recommend?

A. Create three new CloudTrail trails with three new S3 buckets to store the logs one for the AWS Management console, one for AWS SDKs and one for command line tools. Use IAM roles and S3 bucket policies on the S3 buckets that store your logs
B. Create a new CloudTrail with one new S3 bucket to store the logs. Configure SNS to send log file delivery notifications to your management system. Use IAM roles and S3 bucket policies on the S3 bucket that stores your logs
C. Create a new CloudTrail trail with one new S3 bucket to store the logs and with the global services option selected. Use IAM roles S3 bucket policies and Multi Factor Authentication (MFA) Delete, on the S3 bucket that stores your logs
D. Create a new CloudTrail trail with an existing S3 bucket to store the logs and with the global services option selected. Use S3 ACLs and Multi Factor Authentication (MFA) Delete, on the S3 bucket that stores your logs

219. Which of the following bucket policies will ensure the encryption of objects that are uploaded to a bucket called ' demo. '?

A. {
    "Version":"2012-10-17"
    "Id":"PutObj"
    "Statement": [
    {
    "Sid":"DenyUploads",
    "Effect":"Deny",
    "Principal":"*",
    "Action":"s3:PutObject",
    "Resource":"arn:aws:s3:::demo/*",
    "Condition":{
    "StringNotEquals":{
    "s3:x-amz-server-side-encryption":"aws-kms"
    }
    }
    }
    ]
    }

B. {
    "Version":"2012-10-17"
    "Id":"PutObj"
    "Statement": [
    {
    "Sid":"DenyUploads",
    "Effect":"Deny",
    "Principal":"*",
    "Action":"s3:PutObject",
    "Resource":"arn:aws:s3:::demo/*",
    "Condition":{
    "StringEquals":{
    "s3:x-amz-server-side-encryption":"aws-kms"
    }
    }
    }
    ]
    }

C. {

"Version":"2012-10-17"

"Id":"PutObj"

"Statement": [

{

"Sid":"DenyUploads",

"Effect":"Deny",

"Principal":"*",

"Action":"s3:PutObject",

"Resource":"arn:aws:s3:::demo/*",

}

]

}

D. {

"Version":"2012-10-17"

"Id":"PutObj"

"Statement": [

{

"Sid":"DenyUploads",

"Effect":"Deny",

"Principal":"*",

"Action":"s3:PutObjectEncrypted",

"Resource":"arn:aws:s3:::demo/*",

}

]

}

220. Your CTO believes that your AWS account has been hacked. What is the only way to know for sure if there has been an unauthorized access and what has been done, assuming that your hackers are very sophisticated AWS engineers and doing their best to cover their tracks.

A. Use AWS Config SNS Subscriptions and process events in real time

B. Use AWS Config Timeline forensics

C. Use CloudTrail Log File Integrity Validation

D. Use CloudTrail backed up to AWS S3 and Glacier

221. Identify the correct sequence of KMS; how it manages the keys when used in conjunction with the Redshift cluster service?
    A. The master keys encrypt the database key. The database key encrypts the data encryption keys
    B. The master keys encrypt the cluster key. The cluster key encrypts the database key. The database key encrypts the data encryption keys
    C. The master keys encrypt the data encryption keys. The data encryption keys encrypt the database key
    D. The master keys encrypt the cluster key, database key and data encryption keys

222. An application is designed to run on an EC2 instance, which should work with a bucket S3. In the security context, what is the ideal way to set up the EC2 instance / application?
    A. Assign an IAM group and assign it to the EC2 Instance
    B. Assign an IAM user to the application that has specific access to only S3 bucket
    C. Use the AWS access keys ensuring that they are frequently rotated
    D. Assign an IAM Role and assign it to the EC2 Instance

223. You are designing a connectivity solution between on - site infrastructure and Amazon VPC. On - site communication with your VPC instances will take place on your server. You are setting up IPSec tunnels over the internet. On AWS - supported customer gateways, you will use VPN gateways and terminate the IPsec tunnels. By implementing an IPSec tunnel as outlined above, which of the following goals would you achieve? (Choose 4 answers)
    A. Peer identity authentication between VPN gateway and customer gateway
    B. End-to-end protection of data in transit
    C. Protection of data in transit over the Internet
    D. End-to-end Identity authentication
    E. Data integrity protection across the Internet
    F. Data encryption across the Internet

224. A company has a set of AWS - hosted EC2 instances. There are volumes of EBS for these instances to store critical information. There is a requirement for business continuity and to boost business agility and ensure data durability. Which of the options are required? (Choose 2 answers)
    A. Use EBS volume encryption

B. Use lifecycle policies for the EBS volumes

C. Use EBS Snapshots

D. Use EBS volume replication

225. You need to set up a secure solution for your company to backup and archive, using AWS. Documents should be available for three months immediately and for five years for reasons of compliance. Which AWS service meets the requirements, cost - effectively?

   A. Use Direct Connect to upload data to S3 and use IAM policies to move the data into Glacier for long-term archiving

   B. Use Storage Gateway to store data to S3 and use lifecycle policies to move the data into Redshift for long-term archiving

   C. Upload the data on EBS, use lifecycle policies to move EBS snapshots into S3 and later into Glacier for long-term archiving

   D. Upload data to S3 and use lifecycle policies to move the data into Glacier for long-term archiving

226. The AWS EC2 and ELB for Web applications are planned by your company. The security policy requires the encryption of all traffic. Which of the following options ensure that it is fulfilled? (Choose 2 answers)

   A. Ensure that the HTTPS listener sends requests to the instances on port 443

   B. Ensure that the load balancer listens on port 443

   C. Ensure that the HTTPS listener sends requests to the instances on port 80

   D. Ensure that the load balancer listens on port 80

227. Your team is testing for an application using the API gateway service. A custom module needs to be implemented to authenticate / authorize calls to the API gateway. How would you do that?

   A. Use the gateway authorizer

   B. Use the request parameters for authorization

   C. Use a Lambda authorizer

   D. Use CORS on the API gateway

228. Your S3 bucket contains private video content that you want to serve on the Internet to the subscribed users. User IDs, credentials and subscriptions are stored in an Amazon RDS database. Which configuration will enable you to securely serve your users the private content?

A. Create an IAM user for each subscribed user and assign the Get Object permission to each IAM user

B. Create an S3 bucket policy that limits access to your private content to only your subscribed users' credentials

C. Create a CloudFront Origin Identity user for your subscribed users and assign the GetObject permission to this user

D. Generate pre-signed URLs for each user as they request access to protected S3 content

229. Your company examines the gaming domain and hosts several game servers as EC2 Instances. Each server serves thousands of users. 1. The attacks by DDos on the EC2 instances could lead to a big loss of revenue. Which of following may help to mitigate this security issue and also ensure minimum server downtime?

A. Use AWS Shield Advanced to protect the EC2 Instances

B. Use VPC Flow logs to monitor the VPC and then implement NACL's to mitigate attacks

C. Use AWS Trusted Advisor to protect the EC2 Instances

D. Use AWS Inspector to protect the EC2 Instances

230. The following AWS setup is provided by your company:
    - A set of EC2 Instances hosting a web application
    - An Application Load Balancer placed in front of the EC2 Instances

    A number of malicious requests from a number of IP addresses appear. To protect against these requests, which of the following can be applied?

A. Use AWS WAF to block the IP addresses

B. Use AWS Inspector to block the IP addresses

C. Use VPC Flow Logs to block the IP addresses

D. Use Security Groups to block the IP addresses

231. Your company recently installed a new VPC central server. Other teams with servers located on various VPCs in the same region are required to connect to the central server. Which of the following options are best suited for this?

A. Setup AWS DirectConnect between the central server VPC and each of the team's VPCs

B. Setup an IPSec Tunnel between the central server VPC and each of the team's VPCs

C. Setup VPC peering between the central server VPC and each of the team's VPC.

D. None of the above options will work

232. For your AWS Account, your company defines privileged users. These users are managers for the company's key resources. A mandate to improve the safety authentication of these users is now a requirement. How can this be done?

A. Enable MFA for these user accounts

B. Disable root access for the users

C. Enable accidental deletion for these user accounts

D. Enable versioning for these user accounts

233. There is an external website for your company. The objects in the S3 bucket must be accessed from this site. Which of the following options would allow the website to access the objects in the safest way?

A. Use the aws:sites key in the condition clause for the bucket policy

B. Grant public access for the bucket via the bucket policy

C. Use the aws:Referer key in the condition clause for the bucket policy

D. Grant a role that can be assumed by the web site

234. A company's CFO would like to allow one of its employees to view the AWS usage report page. Which of the IAM policy statements mentioned below allow the user to access the AWS usage report page?

A. "Effect":"Allow", "Action": ["aws-portal:ViewUsage"," aws-portal:ViewBilling"],"Resource": "*"

B. "Effect":"Allow", "Action": ["aws-portal: ViewBilling"], "Resource": "*"

C. "Effect": "Allow", "Action": ["Describe"],"Resource": "Billing"

D. "Effect":"Allow", "Action": ["AccountUsage], "Resource": "*"

235. A company plans to use AWS to host their applications. They want their production, testing and development environments to be completely separated and isolated. Which of the following is the perfect way to create such setup?

A. Use separate IAM Policies for each of the environments

B. Use separate AWS accounts for each of the environments

C. Use separate IAM Roles for each of the environments

D. Use separate VPC's for each of the environments

236. Your company has ordered the encryption of all data in AWS, at rest. How can this be achieved for EBS volume? (Choose 2 answers)
    A. Boot EBS volume can be encrypted during launch without using custom AMI
    B. Use AWS Systems Manager to encrypt the existing EBS volumes
    C. Use TrueCrypt for EBS volumes on Linux instances
    D. Use Windows bit locker for EBS volumes on Windows instances

237. Your company is hosting its resources using AWS. They have the following requirements:
    - Facility to allow auditing credentials and logins
    - Help in understanding what resources are there in the account
    - Record all API calls and Transitions
    Which services would meet the requirements mentioned above?
    A. AWS SQS, IAM Credential Reports, CloudTrail
    B. AWS Inspector, CloudTrail, IAM Credential Reports
    C. CloudTrail, IAM Credential Reports, AWS SNS
    D. CloudTrail, AWS Config, IAM Credential Reports

238. Your developer uses the KMS service and assigned key in their Java program. While running the code, they get the following error:
    arn:aws:iam::113745388712:user/UserB   is   not   authorized   to   perform: kms:DescribeKey
    Which of the following might help solve the problem?
    A. Ensure that UserB is given right permissions in the Key policy
    B. Ensure that UserB is given the right permissions in the Bucket policy
    C. Ensure that UserB is given right permissions in the IAM policy
    D. Ensure that UserB is given right IAM role to access the key

239. The AWS KMS service was used by a company to manage its keys. They plan to perform housekeeping activities and remove keys that are no longer in use. What are the ways in which you can incorporate the keys in use?
    A. Use AWS CloudWatch events for events generated for the Customer Master Key
    B. See Cloudtrail for usage of the Customer Master Key
    C. See who is assigned permissions to the Customer Master Key
    D. Determine the age of the Customer Master Key

240. Your CTO is very concerned about your AWS account's security. How can you prevent hackers from hijacking your account completely?
    A. Use AWS IAM Geo-Lock and disallow anyone from logging in except for in your city
    B. Use MFA on all users and accounts, especially on the root account
    C. Do not write down or remember the root account password after creating the AWS account
    D. Use short but complex password on the root account and any administrators

Answers

1. **B** (There is a limit on KMS API calls)

Explanation:

The requests are being throttled primarily because there is a limit on the number of calls to KMS.

2. **A** (Use the AWSLambdaKinesisExecutionRole)

   C (Create a service role of the type AWS Lambda)

Explanation:

This is given as the steps in the AWS documentation. Since the roles are clearly given in the documentation, all other options are incorrect.

3. **B** (Kms:Decrypt)

   C (Kms:GenerateDataKey)

Explanation:

If Kinesis Firehose needs to access an S3 bucket, where encryption is enabled using KMS, then the options need to be present in the policy are clearly mentioned in AWS documentation.

4. **D** (Ensure that the policy applied to the users has access to DynamoDB and CloudWatch)

Explanation:

If you are developing an application using Kinesis Client Library (KCL), your policy must include permissions for Amazon DynamoDB and Amazon CloudWatch.

5. **A** (Enable server-side encryption for Kinesis streams)

Explanation:

The easiest way is to use the in-built server-side encryption available with Kinesis streams.

6. **C** (Use CloudTrail logs)

Explanation:

Amazon Kinesis Data Streams are integrated with AWS CloudTrail. CloudTrail captures API calls made on your behalf and delivers log files to your specified Amazon S3 bucket.

7. **A** (Enable enhanced monitoring for the stream)

Explanation:

Shard level data is sent every minute for an additional cost. To get this level of data, you specifically enable it for the stream using the EnableEnhancedMonioring operation.

8. **A** (Use a VPC endpoint interface)

Explanation:

You can use an interface VPC endpoint to keep traffic between your VPC and Kinesis Data Streams from leaving the Amazon network. Interface VPC endpoints do not require an internet gateway, NAT device, VPN connection, or AWS DirectConnect connection.

9. **A** (Kinesis:GetShardIterator)

   B (Kinesis:DescribeStream)

   C (Kinesis:GetRecords)

Explanation:

Since data is being read from the stream and not put in the stream; the permission of Kinesis:PutRecords is not required.

10. **B** (PutRecord)

   D (DescribeStream)

Explanation:

The DescribeStream action is required before attempting to write records, the producer should check if the stream exists and is active. The PutRecord action is required to write records to the Kinesis stream.

11. **B** (Allow permission for kms:Decrypt)

   D (Allow permissions to ssm:GetParameter)

Explanation:

Following is an example policy that allows the user to call the Systems Manager GetParameter operation on all parameters in the /ReadableParameters path, and the user

is allowed to call the AWS KMS Decrypt operation on the specified customer managed CMK.

```
{
    "Version": "2012-10-17",
    "Statement": [
        {
            "Effect": "Allow",
            "Action": [
                "ssm:GetParameter*"
            ],
            "Resource": "arn:aws:ssm:us-west-2:111122223333:parameter/ReadableParameters/*"
        },
        {
            "Effect": "Allow",
            "Action": [
                "kms:Decrypt"
            ],
            "Resource":        "arn:aws:kms:us-west-2:111122223333:key/1234abcd-12ab-34cd-56ef-1234567890ab"
        }
    }
}
```

12. **B** (Use the CMK key to encrypt the files)
   C (Create a new CMK in AWS KMS)

Explanation:

AWS provides an encryption client, which is embedded into the AWS SDK and CLI. With client-side encryption using KMS, the customer creates a CMK in KMS associated with the key id.

13. **C** (Each CMK key can have multiple Alias' point to it)
   D (The alias key must be unique in the AWS account and region)

Explanation:

Each CMK can have multiple aliases, but each alias points to only one CMK. The alias name must be unique in the AWS account and region. To simplify code that runs in

multiple regions, you can use the same alias name but point it to a different CMK in each region.

14. **D** (Allow actions on kms:Encrypt, kms:Decrypt, kms:ReEncrypt*, kms:GenerateDataKey*, kms:DescribeKey)

Explanation:

Key policies are the primary way to control access to Customer Master Keys (CMKs) in AWS KMS. They are not the only way to control access, but you cannot control access without them.

15. **B** (Create a VPC endpoint interface and make the application use the VPC gateway)

Explanation:

You can connect directly to AWS KMS through a private endpoint in your VPC instead of connecting over the internet. When you use a VPC endpoint, communication between your VPC and AWS KMS is conducted entirely within the AWS network.

16. **C** (Use CloudTrail logs to see all the keys that have been used)

Explanation:

When you use imported key material, you remain responsible for the key material while allowing AWS KMS to use a copy of it. You might choose to do this for one or more of the following reasons:

- To prove that you generated the key material using a source of entropy that meets your requirements
- To use key material from your own infrastructure with AWS services, and to use AWS KMS to manage the lifecycle of that key material within AWS
- To set an expiration time for the key material in AWS and to manually delete it, but to also make it available again in the future. In contrast, scheduling key deletion requires a waiting period of 7 to 30 days, after which you cannot recover the deleted CMK

17. **A** (Use SNS to send notifications)
    D (Use CloudTrail service for monitoring the API usage)

Explanation:

CloudTrail logs all KMS operations, including Read-only operations, such as ListAliases, GetKeyPolicy, operations that manage CMKs such as CreateKey and PutKey operations.

18. **B** (Disable the keys that are not being used)

    C (Use CloudTrail logs to see where all the keys have been used)

Explanation:

Deleting a CMK in KMS is destructive and potentially dangerous. It deletes the key material and all metadata associated with it. It is an irreversible action. CMK should only be deleted when you are sure that you do not need this key anymore. If you are not sure, consider disabling the key instead of deleting it.

19. **D** (Use CloudWatch events)

Explanation:

When you enable annual rotation of CMK's key material, AWS KMS creates new key material for the CMK each year and sends a corresponding event to CloudWatch events.

20. **D** (Enable encryption at rest for the DynamoDB table)

Explanation:

With encryption at rest, DynamoDB transparently encrypts all customer's data in an encrypted table, including its primary key and local and global secondary indexes, whenever the table is persisted to disk.

21. **B** (Use AWS Kinesis Firehose service)

    D (Have an S3 bucket in place for log storage)

Explanation:

You can enable logging to get detailed information about traffic that is analyzed by your web ACL. To get started, you set up an Amazon Kinesis Data Firehose. As part of the process, you choose a destination for storing your logs.

22. **C** (Create a Geographic Match Condition)

Explanation:

If you want to allow or block web requests based on the country that the request originates from, create one or more geo match conditions.

23. **B** (Place a CloudFront distribution in front of the EC2 instances)

    D (Place an Application Load Balancer in front of the EC2 instances)

Explanation:

AWS WAF is a web application firewall that lets you monitor the HTTP and HTTPS requests that are forwarded to Amazon CloudFront or an Application Load Balancer. AWS WAF also lets you control access to your content.

24. **C** (Pay for AWS Shield Advanced service and contact AWS Support Center)
    D (Use the WAF service and set up rules to respond to such attacks)

Explanation:

If DDoS alarms indicate possible layer 7 attack, you have two options:

Investigate and mitigate the attack on your own; if you determine that activity represents a DDoS attack, you can create your own AWS WAF rules to mitigate the attack. AWS WAF is included with AWS Shield Advanced at no additional cost. AWS provides preconfigured templates to get you started quickly. If you are an AWS Shield Advanced customer, you also have the option of contacting the AWS Support Center; if you want assistance in applying mitigations, you can contact the AWS Support Center. Critical and urgent cases are routed directly to DDoS experts. With AWS Shield Advanced, complex cases can be escalated to the DRT, which has deep experience in protecting AWS, Amazon.com, and its subsidiaries.

25. **D** (Consider buying a customized set of rules from the AWS Marketplace)

Explanation:

You can install a single AWS Marketplace rule group from your preferred AWS partner and also add your customized AWS WAF rules for increased protection.

26. **D** (AWS Config)

Explanation:

You can use AWS Config to record configuration changes for CloudFront distribution setting changes.

27. **C** (Use Signed cookies)

Explanation:

Use signed cookies in the following cases

- You want to provide access to multiple restricted files
- You do not want to change your current URLs

28. **C** (Create a destination S3 bucket for the logs)
    D (Enable logging for the distribution)

Explanation:

When you enable logging for a distribution, you specify the Amazon S3 bucket on which CloudFront will store logs. If you are using S3 as origin, it is recommended that you do not use the same bucket for log storage to simplify the management.

29. **A** (Change the permissions on the bucket for the origin access identity has read permissions)
    D (Create an origin access identity)

Explanation:

To ensure that your users access your objects using only CloudFront URLs, regardless of whether the URLs are signed, perform the following tasks:

- Create an origin access identity, which is a special CloudFront user, and associate the origin access identity with your distribution. (For web distributions, you associate the origin access identity with origins, so you can secure all or just some of your Amazon S3 content.)
- Change the permissions either on your Amazon S3 bucket or on the objects in your bucket, so only the origin access identity has read permission (or read and download permission)

30. **C** (Use an SSL certificate)
    D (Change the viewer protocol policy)

Explanation:

If you are using your own domain name, such as example.com, you need to change several CloudFront settings. You also need to use an SSL/TLS certificate provided by AWS Certificate Manager (ACM), import a certificate from a third-party certificate authority into ACM or the IAM certificate store, or create and import a self-signed certificate.

31. **B** (Ensure that the security groups have been set for allowing traffic)
    D (Ensure that the network ACLs have been set for allowing traffic)

Explanation:

If you are deploying and managing your own AD DS installation domain controllers and member servers require several security group rules to allow traffic for services such as

AD DS replication, user authentication, Windows Time services, and Distributed File System (DFS), among others. You should also consider restricting these rules to specific IP subnets that are used within your VPC.

32. C (Enable MFA for your AWS managed MS AD)

Explanation:

You can enable Multi-Factor Authentication (MFA) for your AWS Managed Microsoft AD directory to increase security when your users specify their AD credentials to access Supported Amazon Enterprise Applications. When you enable MFA, your users enter their username and password (first factor) as usual, and they must also enter an authentication code (the second factor) they obtain from your virtual or hardware MFA solution. These factors together provide additional security by preventing access to your Amazon Enterprise applications, unless users supply valid user credentials and a valid MFA code.

33. C (Use password policies in the directory service)

Explanation:

You may also modify the following properties of your password policies to specify if and how Active Directory should lockout an account after login failures:

- Number of failed login attempts allowed
- Account lockout duration
- Reset failed login attempts after some duration

34. D (Use DirectConnect)

Explanation:

Out of all the options, DirectConnect is the only service which does not require the internet and would be faster and securer than VPN/Remote Gateway.

35. C (Enable LDAP over SSL)

Explanation:

To mitigate this form of data exposure, AWS Managed Microsoft AD provides an option for you to enable LDAP over Secure Sockets Layer (SSL)/Transport Layer Security (TLS), also known as LDAPS. With LDAPS, you can improve security across the wire and meet compliance requirements by encrypting all communications between your LDAP-enabled applications and AWS Managed Microsoft AD directory.

36. **D** (Build the application server on a public subnet and the database at the client's data center. Connect them with a VPN connection that uses IPsec.)

Explanation:

As per requirement, they want a database on the datacenter, so the best option is to create a VPN connection between database and server on AWS.

37. **A** (Bucket policies)
   B (Buckets ACL's)

Explanation:

By using bucket policies and bucket ACL, you can assign permission to external AWS accounts.

38. **C** (Enable CloudTrail logging and create an IAM user who has read-only permissions to the required AWS resources, including the bucket containing the CloudTrail logs.)

Explanation:

AWS CloudTrail is a service that enables governance, compliance, operational auditing, and risk auditing of your AWS account. You can log, monitor and keep API events throughout your AWS infrastructure with CloudTrail. CloudTrail provides a history of AWS API calls, including API calls via the AWS Management Console, AWS SDK, toolboxes, and other AWS services.

39. **D** (AWS Cognito)

Explanation:

Amazon Cognito offers web and mobile app authentication, permission and user management. You can sign up by using a username or password directly or by using third parties such as Facebook, Amazon or Google.

40. **C** (Create an Admin IAM user with the necessary permissions)
   D (Delete the root access account)

Explanation:

The root user credentials (i.e., account owner's credentials) for all AWS accounts provide complete access to all account resources. We recommend that you delete your root access keys since you cannot restrict root user credentials. Then create user credentials for daily interaction with AWS for AWS Identity and Access Management (IAM).

41. **C** (Protection of data in transit)

   D (Encryption of data at rest)

Explanation:

As per shared responsibility model protection of data in transit and encryption of data at rest is the customer's responsibility.

42. **C** (Use CloudTrail to see if any KMS API request has been issued against existing keys)

Explanation:

Using the combination of AWS Simple Notification Service (Amazon SNS) and Amazon CloudTrail, you can create an Alarm that notifies you of AWS KMS API requests trying to use a Customer Master (CMK) Key pending removal. In order to determine if you want to delete the deletion, you may wish to cancel the deletion of the CMK if you receive a notification.

43. **B** (Use a host-based intrusion detection system)

   D (Use a third party firewall installed on a central EC2 Instance)

Explanation:

If you want to inspect the packets themselves , then you need to use custom based software. So, use host-based IDS.

44. **A** (Use a Classic Load balancer and terminate the SSL connection at the EC2 Instances)

Explanation:

As there are applications that work with legacy protocols, make sure ELB can also be used on the network layer, and you, therefore, should choose the Classic ELB. Since traffic must be safe until the EC2 Instances, Ec2 Instances should be subjected to SSL termination.

45. **A** (Amazon CloudTrail)

   B (Amazon CloudWatch Logs)

Explanation:

You can monitor, store, and access your log files with Amazon CloudWatch logs from Amazon Elastic Compute Cloud instances, AWS CloudTrail, Route53 and from other sources. The associated log data can then be retrieved from CloudWatch Logs. AWS

CloudTrail is a service, which enables your AWS account to be managed, complied with, audited and controlled. You can log, monitor and maintain your account activity throughout your AWS infrastructure with CloudTrail including actions taken via AWS Manager Console, AWS SDKs, command line tools and other AWS services. CloudTrail provides event history of your AWS account activity. Simplify security analysis, tracking resources and troubleshooting with this event history.

46. **B** (Tag the instance with a production-identifying tag and modify the employee's group to allow only start, stop, and reboot API calls and not the terminate instance call.)

   D (Tag the instance with a production-identifying tag and add resource-level permissions to the employee user with an explicit deny on the terminate API call to instances with the production tag.)

Explanation:

Tags enable you to classify your AWS resources by purpose, owner or environment in different ways. This is useful if you have a lot of the same resources— you can quickly recognize a certain resource on the basis of your tags. Every tag consists of a key and a value that you set optionally.

47. **C** (Ensure that an IAM service role is created)

Explanation:

To allow the local servers to communicate with AWS Systems Manager, you have to ensure that an IAM service role is set up.

48. **A** (The EC2 instance running your WAF software is included in an Auto Scaling group and placed in between two Elastic Load Balancers.)

Explanation:

WAF sandwich is created by placing EC2 instance having WAF software between 2 Elastic Load Balancers.

49. **A** (Use roles that allow a web identity federated user to assume a role that allows access to the RedShift table by providing temporary credentials.)

Explanation:

"When you create such an application, you will make requests for AWS services that must be signed with an AWS access key. We strongly recommend, however, that you do not

incorporate or distribute long - term AWS credentials with Apps, which a user downloads to a device in an encrypted storage area.

50. **D** (Enable server access logging for the bucket)

Explanation:

You can allow access by logging requests for access to your bucket. Details on a single request, such as the requestor, the name of a picket, the request time, the request action, answer status and the error code, are provided in each log record.

51. **C** (SSL from your application)

Explanation:

The connection to the DB instance running with MySql, MariaDB, Amazon Aurora, SQL Server, Oracle, and PostgreSQL can be encrypted with SSL from your application.

52. **C** (Use AWS Config to check for unencrypted EBS volumes)

Explanation:

The encrypted-volumes config rule for AWS Config can be used to check for unencrypted volumes.

53. **C** (The AWS Lambda function does not have appropriate permissions for the bucket)

Explanation:

The most probable reason is that the Lambda functions have not been permitted to make appropriate changes to the S3 bucket.

54. **A** (Make sure that logs are stored securely for auditing and troubleshooting purpose)
     C (Isolate the machine from the network)
     E (Take a snapshot of the EBS volume)

Explanation:

First isolate the instance, so that on other AWS resources no further safety damage can occur. A pleasing investigation by taking a snapshot of EBS Volume. This is not the case when the initial instance is shut down, and a separate data survey is carried out. This means that we have logs already, and we need to ensure that they are safely stored, so that no unauthorized person can access and manipulate them.

55. **B** (Enable server-side encryption on the S3 bucket)

Explanation:

Server-side encryption is about data encryption at rest—that is; Amazon S3 encrypts your data at the object level as it writes it to disks in its data centers and decrypts it for you when you access it. As long as you authenticate your request and you have access permissions, there is no difference in the way you access encrypted or unencrypted objects.

56. **C** (Ensure one Cloudtrail trail is enabled for all regions)

Explanation:

A trail can now be switched on for your AWS account across all regions. Amazon S3 bucket and the optional CloudWatch Log group that you specified will be delivered by CloudTrail from every region. In addition, CloudTrail will build the same trail in the new region when AWS launches a new region. As a result, without any action, you will receive log files with API activity for the new area.

57. **A** (Use multiple AWS accounts, each account for each department)

Explanation:

As they want to manage the AWS accounts of independent department then create an individual account for each department.

58. **C** (Configure the CloudTrail service in each AWS account and have the logs delivered to a single AWS bucket in the primary account and grant the auditor access to that single bucket in the primary account.)

Explanation:

AWS CloudTrail is a service that allows your AWS account to be governed, adhered to, operationally audited and audited. You can log, monitor and retain API events across your AWS infrastructure through CloudTrail. ASS API calls to your account have been recorded by CloudTrail, including calls made via the AWS Administration Console, AWS SDK, command line tools and other AWS services. This history simplifies security analysis, monitoring, and troubleshooting for changes in resources.

59. **A** (Create different Cognito groups, one for the readers and the other for the contributors.)

Explanation:

You can use groups to create a user collection in a user pool, which often takes place to set user permissions. For instance, for users who are readers, contributors, and editors of your site and app, you can create separate groups.

60. **C** (Use the private key to log into the instance)
   D (Create a key pair using putty)

Explanation:

To create your key pair, you can use Amazon EC2. Alternatively, the public key could be imported into the Amazon EC2 via a third-party tool. A name is required for each key pair. Please select a name that you can remember easily. You specify the name of the public key as the key name of Amazon EC2. Amazon EC2 stores the public key only, and you store the private key. Anyone who has a private key can decrypt the information you have so that your private keys can be stored in a safe place.

61. **C** (Use AWS Inspector API in the pipeline for the EC2 Instances)

Explanation:

In your operating systems and applications, Amazon Inspector offers programmed ways of detected security defects or errors. Because API calls are available both to the assessment processing and to the results of your evaluations, it is easy to integrate the results into the workflow and notification systems. DevOps teams can incorporate Amazon Inspector with their CI / CD pipelines and use them to identify problems.

62. **B** (Modify the bucket Policy for the bucket to allow access for the VPC endpoint)

Explanation:

By defining the bucket policy, you can restrict the bucket access for VPC endpoint.

63. **C** (AWS CloudFormation)

Explanation:

Security practitioners can use CloudFormation to create a new, trustworthy environment to conduct more in-depth research quickly. In an isolated setting, the CloudFormation template can set up instances in which forensic teams must identify the cause of the event. This reduces the time it takes to collect necessary instruments, isolate examined systems and ensures that the team works in a clean room.

64. **C** (Use Data key caching)

Explanation:

Caching data key stores data keys and the corresponding cryptographic material. The AWS Encryption SDK searches for a matching data key to the cache when you encrypt or decrypt data. If a match is found, the cached data key is used instead of a new data key. Data key caching can improve performance, reduce costs, and help your application to stay within service limits.

65. **A** (Create a separate forensic instance)

   C (Ensure that the security groups only allow communication to this forensic instance)

Explanation:

One way to isolate an affected EC2 instance for investigation is to place it in a Security Group that only the forensic investigators can access. Close all ports except to receive inbound SSH or RDP traffic from one single IP address from which the investigators can safely examine the instance.

66. **D** (Check the Inbound security rules for the database security group Check the Outbound security rules for the application security group)

Explanation:

Since communication is provided inside and outside the application server to the database server, you have to make sure that only the outbound rules for the application server security groups are checked. And then only the incoming rules for security groups are checked for the database server.

67. **C** (Use CloudWatch metrics and logs to watch for errors)

Explanation:

AWS Lambda monitors Lambda functions automatically on your behalf and reports metrics via Amazon CloudWatch. Lambda logs all the requests that are processed by your function and automatically saves logs generated by your code via Amazon CloudWatch Logs to help you resolve failures in a function.

68. **B** (Ensure that the security group allows Inbound SSH traffic from the IT Administrator's Workstation)

Explanation:

The condition for accessing this EC2 instance from its workstation is that the IT administrator does not have appropriate permissions. To do this, we must allow traffic in the IT administrator's workstation by the EC2 Security Group instance.

69. **C** (AWS DirectConnect)
    D (AWS VPN)

Explanation:

For connecting a private connection between on-premises and AWS, you can use AWS DirectConnect and AWS VPN.

70. **A** (AWS Cloud HSM)
    B (AWS KMS)

Explanation:

Now, FIPS 140-2 is being applied by AWS Key Management Service (KMS) to support validation FIPS 140-2 endpoints, which guarantees independent confidentiality and integrity of your keys by using FIPS 140-2 validation modules. The validated FIPS140-2 HSMs automatically protect all master keys in AWS KMS irrespective of their creation date or origin. In the Amazon Virtual Private Cloud (VPC), AWS CloudHSM has a FIPS 150-2 Level 3 validated single-tenant HSM cluster for storage and use. The authentication mechanism independent of AWS exists for you to exclusively control the use of your keys. You are interacting with keys in your AWS CloudHSM cluster similar to your Amazon EC2 interaction.

71. **B** (Use AWS SSM to patch the servers)
    C (Use AWS Inspector to ensure that the servers have no critical flaws)

Explanation:

Amazon Inspector is an automated safety assessment service that improves the safety and compliance of AWS applications. Amazon Inspector evaluates the vulnerabilities applications or deviations from best practices automatically. Amazon Inspector produces a detailed list of the safety findings that have been prioritized according to the severity level after an assessment. These findings may be reviewed directly or as part of the detailed evaluation reports available via a console or API from Amazon Inspector. Once you have understood the list of servers that need critical updates, the required patches can be corrected by using the SSM tool.

72. **C** (Check the /var/log/amazon/ssm/errors.log file)
    D (Ensure that the SSM agent is running on the target machine)

Explanation:

If commands with the Run Command are not executed properly, the SSM Agent could become a problem. Use this to help solve the agent's problem. View Agent Logs.

The SSM Agent logs the information. The information contained in these files can help you solve problems. /var/log/amazon/ssm/errors.log

73. **C** (You cannot decrypt the data that was encrypted under the CMK, and the data is not recoverable.)

Explanation:

Deletion of the AWS Key Management Service (AWS KMS) Customer Master Key (CMK) is destructive and potentially dangerous. It is irreversible the and it removes the key material and metadata related to CMK. After the CMK is removed, the data encrypted by the CMK can no longer be decrypted, so the data becomes irrecoverable. You should only remove a CMK if you are certain that you no longer have to use it. If you are not sure, do not delete the CMK. If you need to use the deleted CMK later, you can re-enable a deleted CMK.

74. **B** (Create pre-signed URL's)

Explanation:

To create signed URLs or signed cookies, you need at least one AWS account that has an active CloudFront key pair. This account is known as a trusted signer.

75. **A** (Use an appropriate Penetration testing tool)
    C (Get prior approval from AWS for conducting the test)

Explanation:

"For the purpose of performing a penetration test on AWS resources, we must first receive permission from AWS and fill in and approve a request form. The form should contain information regarding instants to be tested, identify expected start / finish dates / times and require you to read and agree to penetration testing and U terms and conditions.

76. **D** (You have not explicitly given access via the key policy)
Explanation:

The default policy is to create keys created in KMS. When KMS has features, the default key policy for these keys needs to be explicitly updated.

77. **C** (Create a new DHCP options set and replace the existing one)

Explanation:

You need to ensure that a new custom DHCP option with the IP of the custom DNS server is created to use your own DNS server. The existing set cannot be changed, so you must create another set.

78. **B** (Use the SSM Run command to send the list of running processes information to an S3bucket.)

Explanation:

This can be done using the SSM Run command to send certain OS commands to an instance. You can check and view, on an instance, the running processes and then send the output to an S3 bucket.

79. **A** (Configure AWS as the relying party in Active Directory Federation services)
    C (Ensure the right match is in place for On-premise AD Groups and IAM Roles)

Explanation:

Determining how you create and describe your AD groups and IAM roles in AWS is important in ensuring access and management of your account. The AWS environment and the respective IAM roles are managed via regular (regex) expression matching the AWS IAM function with the name of your AD group on the premises. The selection of a common group naming convention is one way of creating AD groups that uniquely identify the AWS IAM role mapping. For instance, your AD groups start with an identification, such as AWS, because it differentiates your AWS groups from others in the organization. The AWS account number is 12-digits. Finally, inside the AWS account, add a matching role name. And next is the configuration of the relying party, which is AWS ADFS federation, made with the participation of two parties; the identity or claims provider and the trusted party, which is an additional request that wants authentication to be external to the identity provider; in this case Amazon Secure Token Service (STS) is one of the involved parties. ADFS federation is the one with the identity or claims provider. The relying party is a partner of the federation represented in federal service by a claims provider trust.

80. **C** (Search the Cloudtrail event history on the API events which occurred 15 days ago.)

Explanation:

Events recorded for 90 days can be viewed in the Cloud Trail history. So you can use a metric filter to collect 15 days ago API calls.

81. **D** (Use VPC Flow logs to get the IP addresses accessing the EC2 Instances)

Explanation:

You can find the list of IP addresses in your VPC using VPC Flow logs. Use the logs to see which external IP addresses send a bunch of requests that may pose a potential threat to a DDoS attack. VPC Flow logs are the feature to capture information about the IP traffic going to and from VPC's network interface.

82. **B** (The response plan does not cater to new services)

Explanation:

Therefore, the incident response plan does not cover the services that have been newly created. AWS continues to change and add new services, and therefore these new services need to be covered by the Response Plan.

83. **C** (Provide the ARN for the role to the partner account)
    D (Ensure the partner uses an external id when making the request)
    F (Ensure an IAM role is created which can be assumed by the partner account)

Explanation:

Ensure that the partner uses an external Id when making the request. Give the ARN to the partner account. Make sure that the partner uses an external ID for the request. All these need to ensure that it allows partner account to access your account S3 bucket.

84. **C** (Create a database security group and ensure the web security group to allow incoming access)
    D (Place the EC2 Instance with the Oracle database in a separate private subnet)

Explanation:

As they want Oracle DB EC2 instance so for that, DB is created to serve in private subnet with a security group that ensures the web security group to allow incoming access and not allowing traffic from the internet.

85. **C** (Configuring lifecycle configuration rules on the S3 bucket)

Explanation:

The configuration of the lifecycle allows you to specify the management cycle of objects in a bucket. A set of one or more rules is the configuration, where each rule specifies an action for a group of objects for Amazon S3. The following actions can be classified: as transition and expiry actions.

In transition, you define to transition an object to other storage class while in expiration action you define after a particular time that object is deleted form bucket.

86. **B** (Ensure the security groups for the AD hosted subnet has the right rule for relevant subnets)

Explanation:

In addition to the VPC peering and setting the correct route tables, the AD EC2 instance security groups need to ensure that the right traffic rules are implemented.

87. **B** (For the Bucket policy add a condition for {"Null": { "aws:MultiFactorAuthAge":true }})
    D (Enable bucket versioning and also enable CRR)

Explanation:

For region sharing, you need to enable CRR, and Amazon S3 supports a Multi-Factor Authentication (MFA) tool for the access of Amazon's S3 resources to the MFA-protected API access. Multi-factor Authentication offers an additional degree of security for your AWS environment. It is a security feature that requires users to physically prove that an MFA device is available with a valid MFA code.

88. **A** (Check the Instance status by using the Health API)
    B (Ensure that agent is running on the Instances)
    D (Check to see if the right role has been assigned to the EC2 Instances)

Explanation:

First, install the latest version of SSM agent on instance then configure an instance with AWS IAM role to communicate it with System Manager API. Also, use EC2 health API for quickly determine the information about instances like version or status of EC2Config service, version of SSM agent, OS and last instance heartbeat value.

89. **C** (Use SAML (Security Assertion Markup Language) to enable single sign-on between AWS and LDAP.))

Explanation:

You integrate your existing LDAP user directory with AWS and Single Sign-On; integrating AWS, OpenLDAP, and Shibboleth. Users are able to access AWS using their existing credentials when you integrate your existing directory with AWS. So your users do not have to keep another username and password only in order to access AWS resources. For single Sign on you need to use SAML.

90. **D** (Do not do anything since CloudTrail logs are automatically encrypted)

Explanation:

The default is Amazon's server-side encoding of Amazon S3-managed encryption keys (SSE - S3) to your log files delivered by CloudTrail to your bucket.

91. **A** (This is not possible since keys from KMS are region specific)

Explanation:

Keys are only stored and used in the region in which they are created. They cannot be transferred to another region. For example; keys created in the EU-Central (Frankfurt) region are only stored and used within the EU-Central (Frankfurt) region.

92. **B** (Use the kms:ViaService condition in the Key policy)

Explanation:

The kms:ViaService condition key limits use of a customer-managed CMK to requests from particular AWS services. (AWS managed CMKs in your account, such as aws/s3, are always restricted to the AWS services that created them.)

93. **D** (Use IAM Roles with permissions to interact with DynamoDB and assign it to the EC2 Instance)

Explanation:

To always ensure secure access to AWS resources from EC2 Instances, always ensure to assign a Role to the EC2 Instance

94. **C** (Use AWS KMS Customer Default master key)

Explanation:

The hierarchy of encryption keys is used by Amazon Redshift for encrypting the database. The top-level encryption keys in this hierarchy may be managed by using either AWS Key

Management Service (AWS KMS) or a hardware security module (HSM). Depending on how you manage the keys, Amazon Redshift decides the process of encryption.

95. **B** (Put the metadata in a DynamoDB table and ensure that the table is encrypted during creation time.)

Explanation:

When you place an object in S3, and they are encrypted, then its metadata is not encrypted in any case, so you need to put metadata in encrypted DynamoDB table.

96. **C** (Use Systems Manager Patch Manager to generate the report of out of compliance instances/ servers. Use Systems Manager Patch Manager to install the missing patches.)

Explanation:

The AWS Systems Manager Patch Manager automates the patching process with security-related updates of managed instances. You can also set up patches for non-security updates for Linux-based instances. Amazon EC2 instance fleets or your on-site servers and VMs can be patched by operating system type. These include the Windows, Ubuntu Server, Red Hat Enterprise Linux (RHEL), SUSE Linux Enterprise Server (SLES) and Amazon Linux versions that are supported. Instances can be scanned for the missing patches, or all missing patches are scanned and installed automatically.

97. **C** (Use the AWS Trusted Advisor to see which security groups have compromised access.)

Explanation:

The AWS Trusted Advisor could check security groups for rules that allow unrestricted access to a resource. Unrestricted access increases opportunities for malicious activity (hacking, denial-of-service attacks, loss of data).

98. **D** (You have not explicitly given access via the key policy)

Explanation:

By default, keys created in KMS are created with the default key policy. When features are added to KMS, you need to explicitly update the default key policy for these keys.

99. **D** (Enable MFA for these user accounts)

Explanation:

For extra security, enable MFA for privileged IAM users (users who can access sensitive resources or APIs). Enable Multi-Factor Authentication. With MFA, users have a uniquely authenticated device (one-time password, or OTP). Both user credentials (such as username or password) and OTP must be provided by users. The MFA system can be either a special device or a virtual one (for example, it can run on a smartphone in an application).

100. **D** (Conduct an audit on a yearly basis)

Explanation:

A yearly security audit is a long gap so you should audit your security configuration in the following situations:

- If you ever suspect that an unauthorized person might have accessed your account
- If you have added or removed software in your accounts, such as applications on Amazon EC2 instances, AWS OpsWorks stacks, AWS CloudFormation templates, etc
- If you have stopped using one or more individual AWS services. This is important for removing permissions that users in your account no longer need
- If there are changes in your organization, such as people leaving
- On a periodic basis

101. **A** (Use AWS Config to examine the employee's IAM permissions prior to the incident and compare them to the employee's current IAM permissions.)

Explanation:

You can use the AWS Config history to see the history of a particular item.

102. **D** (Shutdown the instance)

Explanation:

It is recommended that the instance is shut down as soon as possible in a test environment to mitigate the risk. Furthermore, the removal of security group rules does not mean that because of a connection error the user is logged out of the EC2.

103. **A** (This is not possible since keys from KMS are region specific)

Explanation:

Keys are only stored and used in the region in which they are created from KMS. They cannot be transferred to another region. For example, keys created in the EU-Central (Frankfurt) region are only stored and used within the EU-Central (Frankfurt) region

104. **A** (Create an IAM service role with permissions to write to the DynamoDB table. Associate that role with the Lambda function.)

Explanation:

To assign permission, IAM role is the best way to choose and associate it with Lambda function. In role, define all required permission for secure access to AWS resource.

105. **D** (Delete the AWS keys for the root account)

Explanation:

A deleted key for the IAM root user is the first level or measure that is to be taken. This is the first step that you can see when you log into your account and access your security access dashboard.

106. **C** (Enable Cloud Trail log file integrity validation)

　　E (Create an S3 bucket in a dedicated log account and grant the other accounts write-only access. Deliver all log files from every account to this S3 bucket.)

Explanation:

You can use CloudTrail log file integrity validation to determine that a log file has been modified, deleted or unchanged after CloudTrail delivers it. This feature is designed using standard industry algorithms: the hashing SHA-256 and digital signing SHA-256 and RSA. This allows it to change, delete or forge log files without detection which is computationally impossible.

107. **B** (Use AWS Inspector)

Explanation:

The AWS Inspector service can inspect EC2 Instances based on specific Rules. One of the rules packages is based on the guidelines set by the Center of Internet Security.

108. **B** (Add permission to use the KMS key to decrypt to the EC2 instance role)

　　C (Add permission to read the SSM parameter to the EC2 instance role)

Explanation:

To read the security string of AWS KMS, the following example policy of AWS Documentation must be provided to the EC2 Instance. Permissions for the Get Parameter API and KMS API call must be granted to decrypt the secret.

```
{
    "Version": "2012-10-17",
    "Statement": [
        {
            "Effect": "Allow",
            "Action": [
                "ssm:GetParameter*"
            ],
            "Resource": "arn:aws:ssm:us-west-2:111122223333:parameter/ReadableParameters/*"
        },
        {
            "Effect": "Allow",
            "Action": [
                "kms:Decrypt"
            ],
            "Resource":        "arn:aws:kms:us-west-2:111122223333:key/1234abcd-12ab-34cd-56ef-1234567890ab"
        }
    ]
}
```

109. **A** (Use AWS Config to get the list of all resources)

Explanation:

The AWS Config facilitates the monitoring of multi-account, multi-region data aggregation capability in multiple accounts and regions. You can create a configuration aggregator and add compliance information from other accounts to any account.

110. **C** (Use VPC Flow logs to diagnose the traffic)

Explanation:

VPC Flow Logs capture and store information about network flows in Amazon CloudWatch Logs for a VPC, a subnet, or network interface. Flow log data can be of

assistance for client network problems; for example, it may be because of excessively restrictive security group rules to diagnose why specific traffic does not reach an instance. The customer can also use flow logs as a security tool for traffic monitoring, network traffic profile and abnormal transport conduct.

111. **B** (Submit a request to AWS Support)

Explanation:

Before performing security testing on AWS resources, you must obtain approval from AWS. After you submit your request, AWS will reply in about two business days.

112. **C** (Use the AWS Trusted Advisor to see which security groups have compromised access.)

Explanation:

The Advisor can check for rules to allow unrestricted access to a resource in security groups. Unrestricted access increases malicious activity opportunities (hacking, denial of service attacks, data loss).

113. **D** (Enable a trail in CloudTrail)

Explanation:

The AWS KMS is integrated with CloudTrail, a system that captures the log files to the bucket Amazon S3 that you entered by, or on behalf of, AWS KMS in your AWS account. Use the Cloud Trail data collected by CloudTrail to identify what request was made; the Source IP address of the request, who made it, when it was made and so on. In this way, CloudTrail captures API calls from either the AWS KMS console or the AWS KMS API.

114. **A** (Use a custom solution available in the AWS Marketplace)

Explanation:

In AWS there is no service for network packet inspection, IDS or IPS, so use custom solution from AWS Market place.

115. **A** (After 3 years)

Explanation:

You cannot handle AWS - managed CMKs with key rotation. Every three years (1095 days), AWS KMS rotates the managed key, automatically.

116. **C** (Create an IAM service role with permissions to write to the DynamoDB table. Associate that role with the Lambda function.)

Explanation:

There is a role associated with each Lambda function (execution role). When creating your Lambda function, you specify the IAM role. You allow AWS Lambda to determine the roles that AWS Lambda can do.

117. **D** (Use a VPC endpoint)

Explanation:

Instead of connecting to the Internet you can connect to AWS KMS by a private endpoint in your VPC. The communication between your VPC and AWS KMS will be carried out completely within the AWS network if you are using a VPC endpoint.

118. **B** (Use Cloud HSM)

Explanation:

CloudHSM allows you to securely generate, store and manage cryptographic keys used for data encryption in a way that keys are accessible only by you.

119. **C** (Enable CORS for the bucket)

Explanation:

By enabling CORS, you can share the resources between the buckets.

120. **C** (There is no need to do anything since the logs will already be encrypted)

Explanation:

By default, files are encrypted by Amazon S3 server-side encryption (SSE) for CloudTrail events. You can choose the AWS Key Management Service (AWS KMS) key to encrypt your log files. Your log files can be saved as long as you want in your bucket. Amazon S3 Lifecycle rules can also be set to archive or automatically delete log files. You can set up Amazon SNS notifications if you want log file notifications and validation.

121. **A** (Change the password for all IAM users)
    C (Rotate all IAM access keys)
    D (Change the root account password)

Explanation:

When any compromised suspect for AWS account and you get a notification then first change your root account password and IAM users' passwords. Delete or rotate all root and IAM access keys. Delete the resources that you do not create.

122. **B** (Shutdown the instance)

    D (Remove the rule for incoming traffic on port 22 for the Security Group)

Explanation:

Security groups in the test environment could be opened for testing purposes to all IP addresses. Always ensure that this rule is removed after all tests have been carried out. Also shutting down the instance is also preferable.

123. **C** (Use Pre-signed URL's)

Explanation:

All items are privately owned by default. The access to these objects is allowed only to the owner of the object. However, by creating a pre-signed URL with its own security credentials, the object's owner may optionally share objects with others to grant time-limited permission, and to download objects.

124. **C** (Change the Resource section to "arn:aws:s3:::appbucket/*".)

Explanation:

You need to ensure that, when you are setting access to objects in a bucket, you specify the items which are to access in a bucket. In such a case, the * may be used to allow all objects in the bucket to be allowed.

125. **B** (Add permission to use the KMS key to decrypt to the EC2 instance role)

    D (Add permission to read the SSM parameter to the EC2 instance role)

Explanation:

In order to read a secure string from AWS KMS, the following example policy from the AWS Documentation is required by the EC2 instance. The Get Parameter API and the KMS API call must be given permissions to decrypt the secret.

```
{
   "Version": "2012-10-17",
   "Statement": [
```

```
        {
            "Effect": "Allow",
            "Action": [
                "ssm:GetParameter*"
            ],
            "Resource": "arn:aws:ssm:us-west-2:111122223333:parameter/ReadableParameters/*"
        },
        {
            "Effect": "Allow",
            "Action": [
                "kms:Decrypt"
            ],
            "Resource":      "arn:aws:kms:us-west-2:111122223333:key/1234abcd-12ab-34cd-56ef-1234567890ab"
        }
    ]
}
```

126. **A** (Use AWS Config to get the list of all resources)

Explanation:

AWS Config is the most feasible option. You'll find a resource list defined in your AWS account when you turn on AWS Config.

127. **A** (Create an IAM policy that gives the desired level of access to the CloudWatch Log group)
   D (Stream the log files to a separate CloudWatch Log group)

Explanation:

You can build a Log Group and send all logs to that group from the EC2 Instance. The Log group access can then be limited via an IAM policy.

128. **B** (Use a Lambda function) and **D** (Create a CloudWatch Events Rule)

Explanation:

Whenever the root user AWS account activity is detected in CloudWatch event rule, it triggers Lambda function and publishes the message by using SNS service.

129. **C** (Consider using AWS Certificate Manager)

Explanation:

ACM is closely connected to the Private Certificate Authority AWS Certificate Manager. You can use ACM PCA to create a CA and use ACM for issuing privately-owned certificates. These are certificates for SSL / TLS X.509, which internally identify the users, computers, applications, services, servers or other devices. Private certificates cannot be publicly trusted.

130. **D** (Enable Cloud Trail log file integrity validation)
    E (Create an S3 bucket in a dedicated log account and grant the other accounts write-only access. Deliver all log files from every account to this S3 bucket.)

Explanation:

You can use CloudTrail log file integrity validation to determine whether a log file has been changed, deleted, or unchanged after CloudTrail delivers it. This feature is made using industry standard algorithms: the hazing SHA-256 and the digital signing SHA-256. This renders CloudTrail log files undetected, computationally unable to be modified, deleted or forged.

131. **B** (Use AWS Inspector)

Explanation:

According to certain rules, the AWS Inspector department can inspect EC2 instances. One of the package regulations is based on the guidelines set by the ISC.

132. **D** (AWS KMS API)

Explanation:

AWS Key Management Service (AWS KMS) is an administered service that makes creating and controlling encryption keys for the encryption of your data easier for you. The AWS KMS is integrated with other AWS services, including Amazon Elastic Block Store, Amazon Simple Storage (Amazon S3), Amazon Redshift, Amazon Elastic Transcoder, Amazon Workmail, Amazon Relational Database Service (Amazon RDS), etc.

133. **C** (db-345- Allow port 1433 from wg-123)
    D (wg-123- Allow ports 80 and 443 from 0.0.0.0/0)

Explanation:

Ports 80 and 443 for HTTP and HTTPS should be accessed by Web security groups for all Internet users. The database security group only should allow access from port 1433 web security group.

134. **D** (Enable MFA for these user accounts)

Explanation:

Enable Multi-Factor Authentication (MFA) for privileged IAM users (users permitted to access sensitive resources or APIs) for additional security. The MFA user has a single authentication code (one-time password, or OTP) to generate a device. Both their user name and password and the OTP must be provided by the users. The MFA can be special hardware or a virtual device (for instance, it can run on a smartphone in an application).

135. **C** (AWS WAF)

Explanation:

AWS WAF is a web application firewall that detects malicious web queries for your web applications and blocks them. The AWS WAF allows you to create policies to protect against common web operations such as cross-site scripting and SQL injection. AWS WAF first identifies the resource you need to protect (either an Amazon CloudFront or an Application Load Balancer).

136. **A** (Port 22 coming from 203.0.113.1/32)
    B (Port443 coming from 0.0.0.0/0)

Explanation:

As traffic from HTTPS is required on the Internet for all users, all IP addresses should be opened by port 443. The traffic for port 22 should be limited to an internal subnet.

137. **C** (An Inline Policy)

Explanation:

If you want to keep a strict relationship between policy, and the principal entity to which it is applied, inline policies are useful.

138. **B** (Change the Inbound NACL to deny access from the suspecting IP)

Explanation:

NACL is your VPC's optional safety layer that acts as a traffic controlling firewall for one or more subnetworks. With rules similar to your security groups, you can set up network ACLs to add a further safety layer to your VPC.

139. **A** (sgLB: Allow port 80 and 443traffic from 0.0.0.0/0 sgWeb: Allow port 80 and 443 traffic from sgLB sgDB: Allow port 3306 traffic from sgWeb and sgBastion sgBastion: Allow port 22traffic from the corporate IP address range)

Explanation:

The load balancer must accept port traffic 80 and 443 of 0.0.0.0/0; Backend EC2 Instances are to accept traffic from the load balancer, the database must allow traffic from the web server and only a specific company IP address, which is permitting traffic from the Bastion host.

140. **A** (Create an IAM role that establishes a trust relationship between IAM and the corporate directory identity provider (IdP))

  B (Create a Direct Connect connection between the on-premise network and AWS. Use an AD connector for connecting AWS with on-premise active directory.)

Explanation:

For access to AWS account to users, you can use AWS Direct Connect connection or define the right IAM role between IAM and organization Idp for federation.

141. **C** (Use IAM Policies to create different policies for the different types of users.)

Explanation:

The control access to API gateway can be done by assigning right IAM permission.

142. **B** (Access the S3 bucket through a VPC endpoint for S3)

Explanation:

VPC endpoint can connect your VPC privately, without the requirement of an internet gateway, NAT device, VPN connection or AWS Direct Connection, to support AWS services and VPC Endpoint services via PrivateLink. Public IP addresses are not necessary to communicate with resources in the service for instances within your VPC. Amazon network does not leave traffic between your VPC and other AWS services.

143. **A** (Upload the file to the company's S3 bucket)

  D (Add a grant to the object's ACL giving full permissions to bucket owner)

Explanation:

An owner of a bucket can upload objects from other AWS accounts. These items are owned and created by the accounts. The owner of the bucket does not possess the objects that are not made by the owner. The bucket owner should therefore first grant authorization to the bucket owner to access these objects using an ACL object. The owner of the bucket can then delegate such permissions through a bucket policy. The bucket owner delegates users' permission on his own account in this example.

144. **C** (Create an Origin Access Identity (OAI) for CloudFront and grant access to the objects in your S3 bucket to that OAI.)

Explanation:

You may want to prevent users from accessing your Amazon S3 objects using Amazon S3 URLs then using CloudFront signed URLs and cookies to provide access to objects on your Amazon S3 bucket. For example, if users access your objects directly in Amazon S3, they will circumvent the controls provided by signed URLs or by signing cookies to control your time and date, which means that a user can no longer access your content. Furthermore, CloudFront logs are not so useful because they are not complete if users access the objects via both CloudFront and directly through Amazon S3 URLs.

145. **C** (Use the AWS Systems Manager Run Command)

Explanation:

You can remotely and securely manage the setup of your managed instances by the AWS Systems Manager Run Command. A managed instance is any Amazon EC2 instance or on-site machine that is configured for Systems Manager in your hybrid environment. Run Command allows you to automate common administrative tasks and make ad hoc changes to the configuration scale. The AWS Console, the AWS Command Line Interface, the Windows PowerShell Tools, or the AWS SDK are possible to operate using Run Command. No additional costs are offered for Run Command.

146. **B** (Use CloudFront and AWS WAF to prevent malicious traffic from reaching the application)
    D (Use an ELB Application Load Balancer and Auto Scaling group to scale to absorb application layer traffic.)

Explanation:

To avoid a DDoS attack, you can use multiple AWS services like AWS CloudFront, Route53, WAF and ELB, and AutoScaling.

147. **C** (Send the local text log files to CloudWatch Logs and configure a CloudWatch metric filter. Trigger CloudWatch alarms based on the metrics.)

Explanation:

The CloudWatch Logs can be sent to log files. The on-premise servers can also send log files. You can then search for certain values by specifying metrics. And then alarms are created on the basis of those measures.

148. **A** (When storing data in S3, enable server-side encryption)

   D (When storing data in EBS, encrypt the volume by using AWS KMS)

Explanation:

For encryption at rest, you can use server-side encryption in S3, or when you are storing data in ELB, you can use AWS KMS to encrypt.

149. **C** (Key pairs)

Explanation:

Key pair is a mixture of a public key and a private key. You use the private key to create a digital signature, and then AWS uses the corresponding public key to validate the signature. Amazon EC2 and Amazon CloudFront uses key pairs.

150. **A** (Run an Amazon Inspector assessment using the Runtime Behavior Analysis rules package against every EC2 instance.)

Explanation:

This option defines "Run Amazon Inspector" using rules for runtime conduct analysis, which will analyze instances behavior and guide how to secure your EC2 instances during an assessment run. The insecure protocol rules of the servers help you determine if your EC2 instance supports unsecured and unencrypted FTP, Telnet, HTTP, IMAP, PoP, versions 3, SMTP, SNMP, and rlogin.

151. **A** (Amazon CloudTrail)

   B (Amazon CloudWatch Logs)

Explanation:

AWS CloudTrail is a service that enables governance, compliance, operational auditing, and risk auditing of your AWS account. With CloudTrail, you can log, continuously monitor, and retain account activity related to actions across your AWS infrastructure. You can access, maintain and monitor your log files with Amazon CloudWatch Logs in Amazon Elastic Compute Cloud (Amazon EC2), AWS CloudTrail (AWS), Amazon Route (AMR), etc. The log data from the CloudWatch Logs can then be found.

152. A (Enable Cross region replication for the S3 bucket)

Explanation:

Compliance requirements–Although Amazon S3 stores your data by default across multiple geographically distant availability areas, it may require you to store data even further. Cross-regional replication enables replication of data between remote AWS regions in order to meet these requirements for compliance.

153. B (Import new key material to a new CMK; point the key alias to the new CMK)
  E (Use CLI or console to explicitly rotate CMKs that have imported key material)

Explanation:

For imported key material, automatic key rotation cannot enable in CMK, so import new key material and point key alias towards new CMK. With CLI or console, you have the opportunity to explicitly rotate CMK's, which have imported key.

154. B (Monitor compliance with AWS Config Rules triggered by configuration changes)
  C (Trigger a Lambda function from CloudWatch event of event type "Compliance Rules Notification Change" that terminates the non-compliant infrastructure.)

Explanation:

For monitoring the compliance, you can use AWS Config Rules which are triggered by configuration changes. You can also use Lambda to trigger on the basis of CloudWatch event for terminating the non-compliance infrastructure.

155. C (Disable the keys)

Explanation:

The removal in AWS Key Management (AWS KMS) of a Customer Master Key (CMK) is destructive and potentially dangerous. It is irreversible and it removes the key material and metadata linked to the CMK. After a CMK is deleted, the data encrypted under that CMK can no longer be uncovered, meaning the data can no longer be recovered. Only if

you are sure, you no longer have to use a CMK then you should delete it. If you are not sure, please deactivate the CMK rather than delete it. If you need to use it later, but cannot recover a deleted CMK, you can reactivate a disabled CMK.

156. **A** (Ensure that a lifecycle policy is defined on the S3 bucket to move the data to Amazon Glacier after 6 months.)
    B (Enable CloudTrail logging in all accounts into S3 buckets)
Explanation:
With CloudTrail you can publish all logs in S3 bucket. For the archival process, you define lifecycle policy to move from S3 to Glacier, after 6 months.

157. **C** (A security group with a rule that allows outgoing traffic on port 443)
    E (A network ACL with rules that allow outgoing traffic on port 443 and incoming traffic on ephemeral ports)
Explanation:
As traffic from the Instance to Port 443 must flow from the Port 443 to a Web service, both network and security regulations must permit outbound traffic. Traffic should be permitted to enter the operating system ephemeral ports on the instance in order to establish a connection on any desired or available port.

158. **B** (AWS Trusted Advisor)
Explanation:
With AWS Trusted Advisor you can monitor the service limits.

159. **A** (Check the Route tables for the VPC's)
Explanation:
You need to make sure that the route tables are changed to allow traffic flow between the VPCs after the VPC peer connection has been established.

160. **D** (Conduct an audit on a yearly basis)
Explanation:
On a yearly basis conducting security, the audit is not a good best practice.

161. **C** (Trigger a Lambda function with a monthly CloudWatch event that creates a new CMK and updates the S3 bucket to use new CMK.)

Explanation:

You can create a new key using Lambda and then update the S3 bucket with the new key. Do not remove the old key. Otherwise, the document stored in the S3 bucket cannot be decrypted using the older key.

162. **B** (Use IAM user policies)

    C (Use Bucket policies)

Explanation:

Amazon S3 offers options for access policies; widely classified as resource-based policies and user policies. You are referred to resource-based policies when you need to maintain access policies (buckets and objects) to your resources. For example, resource-based policies are bucket policies and Access Control Lists (ACLs). In your account, you can also attach user access policies. These are referred as user policies. You can choose to use resource-based policies or user policies to manage permissions to the resources of your Amazon S3.

163. **C** (Consider moving the database server to a private subnet)

Explanation:

For users on the web, the ideal setup is to ensure that the web server is hosted in the public subnet. In a private subnet, the database server can be hosted.

164. **C** (A VPN between the VPC and the data center over a Direct Connect connection)

Explanation:

Since this is necessary via a low latency consistency connection, a direct connection should be used. You can use a VPN for encryption.

165. **C** (Use AWS Config Rules to check whether logging is enabled for buckets)

Explanation:

With AWS Config rules you can check the logging; either it is enabled or not.

166. **B** (Import the public key into EC2)

    C (Create a new key pair using the AWS CLI)

    D (Use a third party tool to create the Key pair)

Explanation:

For launching an EC2 instance, you can create your own key pair via using the public key, third-party tool or AWS CLI.

167. **C** (Do not save your API credentials, instead create a role in IAM and assign this role to an EC2 instance, when you first create it.)

Explanation:

Rather than saving API credentials, you can create IAM roles to securely request an API by your applications without requiring you to manage the applications' security credentials.

168. **D** (Create a Service Control Policy that denies access to the services. Assemble all production accounts in an organizational unit. Apply the policy to that organizational unit.)

Explanation:

As the master account administrator of an organization, the user and roles of each member account can restrict AWS services and individual API actions. This restriction even overrides the member account managers in the company. If AWS Organizations block the member account's access to a service, user, or role in that account, even if the administrator of a member account explicitly grants those permissions in an IAM policy, it is not possible for any prohibited service or API action to perform an action. The permissions of the organization exceed the permissions of the account.

169. **B** (Consider using the AWS Shield Advanced Service)

Explanation:

For the use of Amazon EC2, Elastic Load Balancing (ELB), Amazon CloudFront and Route 53 applications, AWS Shield Advanced offers enhanced protection against major, more advanced attacks. AWS Shield Advanced is available for business support and business support customers. AWS Shield Advanced is available. AWS Shield Advanced protection provides continuous, flow-based network traffic monitoring and active application monitoring to ensure that DDoS attacks are reported near real time. AWS Shield Advanced also allows customers to take action immediately with very flexible controls on attack mitigations. The DDoS Response Team (DRT) 24X7 can also be used to manage and mitigate their request.

170. **D** (Delete the AWS keys for the root account)

Explanation:

The first level of protection of AWS account is to delete the keys for IAM root user.

171. **C** (Create a Cross Account IAM Role which can be assumed.)

Explanation:

You share resources in a single account with users in a different account. By using setting up cross-account access in this manner, you do not want to create individual IAM users in every account. In addition, users do not need to sign out of one account and sign into every other, which will access resources which are in distinctive AWS accounts. After configuring the role, you understand how to use the role from the AWS Management Console, the AWS CLI, and the API.

172. **A** (Allows access to all AWS resources from workstations in the IP range of 152.0.2.0/24.)

Explanation:

This example shows how you might create a policy that denies access to all AWS actions in the account, when the request comes from outside the specified IP range.

173. **B** (Delete any Access keys which are present for the root account.)

 C (Have a rotation policy in place for changing the root account password.)

Explanation:

We strongly propose that you do not use the root user for your normal tasks, even the administrative ones. Instead, follow the best exercise of the usage of the root user only to create your first IAM user. Then securely lock away the root user credentials and use them to perform only a few account and service management tasks.

You can create, rotate, disable, or delete access keys (access key IDs and secret access keys) on your AWS account root user. You can additionally change your root user password. Everybody who has root user credentials in your AWS account has unrestricted access to all of the resources in your account, including billing statistics.

174. **C** (Create an IAM Role with the right permissions and add it to the EC2 Instance.)

Explanation:

Applications must need to sign their API requests with their AWS credentials. Consequently, if you are an application developer, you need a method for dealing with credentials on your applications that run on EC2 instances. For example, you may securely divide your AWS credentials to the instances, and enables the application on those instances to use your credentials in order to sign requests, even as protecting your credentials from different users. However, it is hard to securely distribute credentials to every instance, especially those which AWS creates on your behalf, including Spot instances or instances in Auto Scaling groups. You must also be capable of updating the credentials on every instance while you rotate your AWS credentials.

175. **D** (Use the AWS CloudTrail service.)

Explanation:

For events which consist of ongoing records in your AWS account, consisting of events for IAM and AWS STS, create a trail. A trail enables CloudTrail to deliver log files to an Amazon S3 bucket. By default, when you create a trail inside the console, the trail applies to all regions. The trail logs events from all regions within the AWS partition and delivers the log files to the Amazon S3 bucket, which you specify.

176. **C** (Create an IAM policy with a condition which denies access when the IP address range is not from the organization)

Explanation:

In fact, you can use a Deny condition to prevent the person from logging in from outside.

Option D is invalid because the security group in the IAM policy is not mentioned.

Option A is invalid as security groups do not allow traffic by default.

Option B is invalid because there is no such option in the IAM policy.

177. **B** (It will deny all access to the bucket mybucket)

Explanation:

The policy consists of 2 statements, one is permitting the bucket user mark and the other is denying policy for all other users. The deny permission will override the permit and therefore, no access to the bucket for all users.

Options A, C and D are all invalid because this policy is used to deny all access to the bucket mybucket.

178. **A** (EC2 instances in our private subnet, no EIPs, route outgoing traffic via the NAT)

Explanation:

In order to make EC2 instances very secure, they need to be in a private subnet like the database server with no EIP and all traffic routed via the NAT.

179. **D** (Ensure that the bucket policy has a condition, which involves aws:PrincipalOrgID)

Explanation:

AWS Identity and Access Management (IAM) now makes it easier for you to use the AWS organization of IAM Principals (users and roles) to control access your AWS resources. Some services allow you to specify the accounts, principals and measures. You can access the resource using resource - based policies. Now, in these policies, you can use a new condition key, aws: PrincipalOrgID, to require all principals accessing the resource from an organization's account.

Option A, B and C are invalid because the condition in the bucket policy has to mention aws:PrincipalOrgID

180. **B** (Use AWS VPC Flow Logs)

Explanation:

A flow log record in your flow log represents a network flow. For a specific 5-tuple, each record captures the network flow for a specific capture window. A 5-tuple is a set of five different values that specify the internet protocol (IP) flow source, destination, and protocol.

Options A, C and D are all invalid because these services/tools cannot be used to get the IP addresses, which are accessing the EC2 Instances.

181. **A** (Create an Origin Access Identity (OAI) for CloudFront and grant access to the objects in your S3 bucket to that OAI.)

Explanation:

You may also want to prevent users from accessing your Amazon S3 objects using Amazon S3 URLs if you want to use CloudFront signed URLs or signed cookies to provide access to objects in your Amazon S3 bucket. If users access your objects directly in Amazon S3, they bypass the controls provided by signed URLs or signed cookies provided by CloudFront, such as checking the date and time. A user can no longer access your content and check which IP addresses can be used to access the content. In addition, if

users access objects both through CloudFront and directly by using Amazon S3 URLs then CloudFront access logs are less useful because they are incomplete.

Option C is invalid because you need to create an IAM user and not a CloudFront identity.

Options B and D are invalid, as individual policies and bucket policies cannot be used to limit access via CloudFront.

182. **C** (Create an IAM role for cross-account access, which allows the SaaS provider's account to assume the role and assign it a policy that allows only the actions required by the SaaS application.)

Explanation

You can use roles to delegate access when third parties require access to the AWS resources of your organization. A third party could provide a service to manage your AWS resources. With IAM roles, without sharing your AWS security credentials, you can grant these third parties access to your AWS resources. Instead, by assuming a role you create in your AWS account, the third party can access your AWS resources.

Third parties must provide you with the following information for you to create a role that they can assume:

An external ID to uniquely associate with the role. The external ID can be any secret identifier that is known by you and the third party. The third party must provide this ID when they assume the role.

The permissions that the third party requires to work with your AWS resources are specified in the role's permission policy.

The third party's AWS account ID, you specify their AWS account ID as a principal when you define the trust policy for the role.

You must provide the third party with the role Amazon Resource Name (ARN) after you create the role. To assume the role, they are the ARN of your role.

183. **D** (Provision a Direct Connect connection to an AWS region using a Direct Connect partner)

Explanation:

AWS Direct Connect makes it easy to connect your premises to AWS with a dedicated network. With AWS Direct Connect, you can connect privately between AWS and your data center, office and colocation environment, which in many instances can reduce the costs of your network. In addition, bandwidth throughput can be enhanced.

Options A and B are invalid because they do not reduce the latency of networks.

Options C is invalid because this is only used to connect 2 VPC's.

184. **B** (Bastion hosts allow users to log in using RDP or SSH and use that session to SSH into internal network to access private subnet resources.)

Explanation:

A bastion host is a special purpose computer on a network that is specifically designed and configured to withstand attacks. The computer usually hosts a single application, such as a proxy server, and all other services are removed or restricted to reduce the computer threat. A bastion host is maintained on a public subnet in AWS. Users log in via SSH or RDP to the bastion host and then use that session to manage other private subnets hosts.

Option A is invalid because a bastion host has to be launched into a public subnet.

Option C is invalid because bastion hosts are not used for monitoring.

Options D is invalid because the bastion host needs to sit on the public network.

185. **C** (Use a script to query the creation date of the keys. If older than 2 months, create new access key and update all applications to use it, inactivate the old key and delete it.)

Explanation:

You can use the list - access - keys command of the CLI to get the access keys. This command also returns the keys' "CreateDate." If the CreateDate is older than 2 months, you can delete the keys. The CLI command Returns list - access - keys returns information about the IAM user - related access key IDs. If there is none, an empty list is returned.

Option A is incorrect because you would not rotate the users themselves.

Option B is incorrect because you do not use IAM roles for such a purpose.

Option D is incorrect because you might use a script for such maintenance activities.

186. **B** (Passwords)
     C (RSA keys)

Explanation:

Only the CMK keys can be used to encrypt data with a maximum size of 4 KB. It can therefore be used to encrypt information like passwords and RSA keys.

Option A and D are invalid because only small amounts of data and not large amounts of data can be encrypted using the actual CMK key. The data key must be generated from the CMK key to encrypt large amounts of data

187. **B** (Ensure that the IAM Role has access for read-only to the S3 buckets)
    D (Create an IAM Role in the company's account)

Explanation:

The following general steps are required to share log files between multiple AWS accounts.

Create an IAM role for each account that you want to share log files with.

Create an access policy for each of these IAM roles that allows read - only access to the account with which you want to share the log files.

Have an IAM user assume the appropriate role in each account and retrieve the log files.

Options A and C are invalid because it is a direct 'NO' practice from a security perspective to create an IAM user and then share the IAM user credentials with the vendor.

188. **A** (AWS CloudFront)
    B (AWS Application Load Balancer)

Explanation:

AWS WAF can be deployed on Amazon CloudFront and the Application Load Balancer (ALB). As part of Amazon CloudFront, it can be part of your Content Distribution Network (CDN) to protect your Edge locations resources and content, and as part of the Application Load Balancer, it can protect your web servers that run behind the ALBs.

Options A and B are invalid because only CloudFront and the Application Load Balancer services are supported by AWS WAF.

189. **A** (It is possible to have different encryption keys for different versions of the same object)

Explanation:

You can encrypt the object and send it to S3 if you manage your own encryption keys.

Option B is invalid because you can use your own encryption keys.

Option C is invalid because different encryption keys should ideally be used.

Option D is invalid because encryption works even if you enable versioning.

190. **C** (Define the tags on the test and production servers and add a condition to the IAMpolicy, which allows access to specific tags)

Explanation:

Tags allow you to categorize your AWS resources in various ways e.g. by purpose, owner, or environment. This is useful if you have many similar type resources — you can quickly identify a specific resource based on the tags you have assigned to it.

Option A is invalid because the type of instance does not meet the requirement.

Option B is invalid because it is not recommended.

Option D is invalid because this is an overhead to maintain this in policies.

191. **D** (Use an IAM role which has permissions to the DynamoDB table and attach it to the Lambda function.)

Explanation:

The functions of AWS Lambda use roles to interact with other services of AWS. Use an IAM role that has DynamoDB table permissions and attach it to the Lambda function.

Options A and C are all invalid because access to AWS keys should never be used.

Option B is invalid because the VPC endpoint is used for VPCs.

192. **B** (DDoS attacks)

Explanation:

For standard flood type attacks against SSL, CloudFront has extensive mitigation techniques. CloudFront disables renegotiation to thwart SSL - type attacks.

Options A, C and D are invalid because Cloudfront is specifically used to protect sites against DDoS attacks.

193. **A** (Setup a central logging server that you can use to archive your logs; archive these logs to an S3 bucket for developer-access.)

Explanation:

One important security aspect is never giving access to actual servers, so from a security perspective, Option B, C and D are completely wrong.

A central logging server to archive logs is the best option. Then you can store these logs in S3.

Options B, C and D are all invalid because the developers on the Apache servers should not provide with access.

194. **B** (Create individual IAM users)

    C (Ensure all users have been assigned and are frequently rotating a password, accessID/secret key, and X.509 certificate)

    D (Configure MFA on the root account and for privileged IAM users)

Explanation:

The security status will show the best practices to initiate the first level of security when you go to the security dashboard. Option A is invalid because AWS requires less privileged access for IAM users and groups.

195. **B** (Ensure that a NAT gateway is present to download the updates)

    D (Use the Systems Manager to patch the instances)

Explanation:

Option A is invalid since the instances must remain in the private subnet.

Option C is invalid because only patches can be detected by AWS inspector.

196. **D** (Use the AWS Encryption CLI to encrypt the data first)

Explanation:

One can use the AWS Encryption CLI to encrypt the data before sending it across the S3 bucket.

Options A and B are not valid as this would still mean transferring data in plain text.

Option C is invalid as the client-side encryption for the S3 bucket cannot be enabled.

197. **C** (Based upon their role, use the IAM groups and add users to different groups and apply the policy to groups)

Explanation:

Option A is wrong because the approach is not ideal.

Option B is wrong because multiple users are not assigned to a policy.

Option D is wrong because you do not add an IAM role user.

An IAM group is used to collectively manage users who need the same set of permissions. By having groups, it becomes easier to manage permissions. This will affect all users in that group if you change the permissions on the group scale.

198. **B** (Use S3 SSE and use SSL for data in transit)

Explanation:

You leave an unsafe connection from the ELB to the back end instances by disabling SSL termination. Therefore, that part of the transit data is not encrypted.

Option A is wrong as this would not ensure that the transit data is completely encrypted.

Option C and D are wrong, because the encryption would not be guaranteed.

199. **A** (AWS Trusted Advisor)

Explanation:

Trusted advisor checks the following security recommendations for compliance:

Limited access to common administrative ports to only a small subset of addresses. This includes ports 22 (SSH), 23 (Telnet) 3389 (RDP), and 5500 (VNC).

Common database ports have limited access. This includes ports 1433 (MSSQL Server), 1434 (MSSQL Monitor), 3306 (MySQL), Oracle (1521) and 5432 (PostgreSQL).

Option B is wrong. Amazon Inspector needs a software agent to be installed on all EC2 instances included in the evaluation target, which you want to evaluate with Amazon Inspector for security. It monitors and collects a broad set of behavior and configuration data (telemetry) of EC2, including network, file system, and processing activity, and passes them to the Amazon Inspector service.

Option C is invalid because these details are not supplied by this service.

Option D is partly correct, but you would have to create custom rules. The Trusted Advisor of AWS can pass all these checks on its dashboard.

A choice that is easy to implement is the requirement of Question. Therefore, Trusted Advisor is the best option.

200. **B** (Enable MFA Delete in the bucket policy)

C (Enable versioning on the S3 bucket)

Explanation:

In the same bucket, the versioning retains many versions of an object. If you enable it, each object in a bucket is automatically fed a unique version ID by Amazon S3. A simple DELETE action does not permanently delete the object version; only a delete marker is associated to the object. You have to specify your version ID in your DELETE request if you want to permanently delete the object version.

By allowing MFA Delete on a versioned bucket, you can add another layer of protection. Once you do, the access keys and a valid code of the MFA device of the AWS account

must be provided so that you can delete a version of an object or suspend or reactivate the bucket version permanently.

Option A is invalid as encryption enables no risk of deletion of data.

Option D is invalid since it does not ensure the risk of deletion of data.

201. **C** (Ensure that there is a trust policy in place for the AWS Config service within the role)

Explanation:

You need to ensure that there is a trust policy in place for the AWS Config service as shown below,

{

"Version":"2012-10-17"

"Statement": [

{

"Sid":"",

"Effect":"Allow",

"Principal":{

"Service":"config.amazonaws.com"

},

"Action":"sts:AssumeRole",

}

]

}

Options A, B and D are invalid because a trust policy is in place and not a policy for grants, users or groups.

202. **A** (Generating the key pairs for the EC2 Instances using puttygen)

Explanation:

You will have complete control of the access keys by ensuring that you generate the key pairs for EC2 Instances.

Options B, C and D are invalid as all these processes mean that the keys are owned by AWS. And the question specifically refers to the need for keys ownership

203. **D** (Use a VPC endpoint to the DynamoDB table)

Explanation:

You can access the DynamoDB service from within a VPC without going to the internet by using VPC endpoints.

204. **D** (Create an OIDC identity provider in AWS)

Explanation:

OIDC Identity Provider are IAM entities that describe a service that supports the OpenID Connect (OIDC) standard as an Identity Provider (IdP). If you want to build trust between an OIDC - compatible IdP — like Google, Salesforce, and many others — and your AWS account, you use an OIDC Identity Provider. This is useful when you create a mobile app or web application that requires access to AWS resources, but you do not want to create customized sign - in code or manage your own user identity.

205. **C** (Monitor the S3 API calls by using CloudTrail logging)

Explanation:

In AWS CloudTrail, Amazon S3 is integrated. CloudTrail is a service that captures specific API calls from your AWS account made to Amazon S3 and delivers the log files to your specified Amazon S3 bucket. It captures API calls made from either the Amazon S3 API or the Amazon S3 console.

You can use the information collected by CloudTrail to determine which request was submitted to Amazon S3, the source IP address from which the request was submitted, who made the request, when it was submitted, etc.

Options A, B and D are invalid because these services cannot be used to get the source IP address of the calls to S3 buckets.

206. **A** (A REJECT record for the response based on the NACL)

    C (An ACCEPT record for the request based on the NACL)

    D (An ACCEPT record for the request based on the Security Group)

Explanation:

For example, you use the ping command from your home computer (IP address is 203.0.113.12) to your instance (the network interface's private IP address is 172.31.16.139). The inbound rules of your security group allow ICMP traffic and the outbound rules do not allow ICMP traffic; however, the response ping from your instance is permitted because security groups are stateful. Your ACL network allows ICMP traffic inbound but does not allow ICMP traffic outbound. Since network ACLs are stateless, the response

ping will be dropped and your home computer will not be reached. This is shown in a flow log as 2 flow log records:

An ACCEPT record for the originating ping that both the ACL network and the security group allows to reach your instance.

An ACCEPT record for the originating ping that was allowed by both the network ACL and the security group, and therefore was allowed to reach your instance.

Option B is invalid because the REJECT record would not be present.

207. **B** (Use CloudWatch events to be triggered for any changes to the Security Groups. Configure the Lambda function for email notification as well.)

Explanation:

Option A and C is invalid because you need to use CloudWatch Events to view changes.

Option D is invalid because AWS inspector is not used to monitor the activity on Security Groups

208. **C** (Add an inline policy for the user)

Explanation:

Option A is invalid because a user is not assigned with IAM role

Options B and D are wrong because you have to include a user - only inline policy

An inline policy is an embedded policy in a principal entity — i.e. the policy is an intrinsic part of the main entity. You can create and incorporate a policy into a main entity, either at the time of creation of the main entity or later.

209. **C** (Modify the Network ACLs associated with all public subnets in the VPC to deny access from the IP Address block.)

Explanation:

NACL acts as a VPC subnet level firewall and we can deny the subnet level offending IP address block, using NACL rules to block incoming traffic to the VPC instances. Since NACL rules are applied in accordance with the rule numbers, ensure that this rule number takes precedence over other rule numbers if there are any rules that allow traffic from these IP ranges. The lowest number of rules has a higher precedence over a rule.

Enable Multi - Factor Authentication (MFA) for privileged IAM users (users are allowed to access sensitive resources or APIs) for additional security. Users have a device with MFA that generates a unique authentication code (one - time password, or OTP). Users must provide their normal credentials (such as their user name and password) as well as

the OTP. The MFA device can either be a special piece of hardware, or it can be a virtual device (such as running on a smartphone in an app).

Option A is invalid because there is no root access for users.

Options B is invalid because these options are not available.

210. **A** (Create another trail that logs management events to another S3 bucket)

B (Create one trail that logs data events to an S3 bucket)

Explanation:

You can configure multiple trails differently so that the trail processes and logs only the events that you specify. For instance, one trail can log read - only data and management events to deliver all read - only events to one bucket. Only write - only data and management events can be logged into another trail, so that all write - only events are delivered to a separate S3 bucket.

Options C and D are invalid because you have to create a trail and not a log group.

211. **C** (Use a network monitoring tool provided by an AWS partner.)

Explanation:

Since the actual network packets need to be sniffed here, the ideal approach would be to use an AWS partner network monitoring tool. Multiple members of the AWS Partner Network offer virtual firewall appliances that can be deployed for inbound or outbound network traffic as an in - line gateway. Additional application - level filtering, deep packet inspection, IPS / IDS and threat protection features of the network are provided by firewall appliances.

Option A is invalid because "promiscuous mode" is not supported in AWS.

Option B and D are invalid because these services cannot be used for packet inspection.

212. **D** (Allow Inbound on port 3306 for Source Web Server Security Group WebSecGrp.)

Explanation:

Because the Web server on port 3306 needs to communicate to the database server, this means that the database server should allow incoming traffic on port 3306.

Options A and B are invalid because you need to allow outbound traffic and not inbound traffic

Option C is invalid because the WebSecGrp security group must allow incoming access to the database server.

213. **A** (Use AWS Systems Manager to patch the servers)

Explanation:

Using Systems Manager Run Command, you can quickly remedy patch and association compliance issues. You can target either Amazon EC2 tags or instance IDs and execute the document AWS - RefreshAssociation or the document AWS - RunPatchBaseline. If you do not resolve the compliance issue by refreshing the association or re - running the patch baseline, then you need to investigate your association's patch baselines or instance configurations to understand why the run command executions did not solve the problem.

Option B is invalid because this service cannot be used to patch servers.

Options C and D are invalid because although this is possible, it would still be difficult to maintain the Lambda functions from a maintenance perspective.

214. **C** (The above command ensures data encryption at rest for the Customer table)

Explanation:

The above command with the "--sse-specification Enabled=true" parameter, ensures that the data for the DynamoDB table is encrypted at rest.

Options A, B and D are invalid because this command is specifically used to ensure data encryption at rest.

215. **B** (Use AWS GuardDuty to monitor any malicious port scans)

Explanation:

GuardDuty voraciously consumes multiple data streams, including multiple threat intelligence feeds, keeping track of malicious IP addresses, devious domains, and more importantly, learning how to accurately identify malicious or unauthorized behavior in your AWS. Combined with information gleaned from your VPC Flow Logs, AWS CloudTrail Event Logs, and DNS logs enable GuardDuty to detect many different types of hazardous and mischievous behaviors, including known vulnerability samples, port scans and probes, and access from unusual locations. On the AWS part it will look for suspicious activity in the AWS account, such as unauthorized deployments, extraordinary CloudTrail activity, patterns of access to AWS API functions and multiple service limit attempts. GuardDuty will also look for affected EC2 instances that talk to malicious organizations or services, data exfiltration attempts and mining cryptocurrency instances.

216. **C** (Use AWS Cognito to manage the user profiles)

Explanation:

In Amazon Cognito, a user pool is a user directory. You can sign in via Amazon Cognito using a user pool to connect to your web or mobile app. Your users can also register by social identity providers, such as Facebook or Amazon, and SAML. All members of the user pool have a Directory profile that can be accessed via an SDK, whether you sign in directly or via a third party.

User pools provide:

A built-in, customizable web UI to sign in users.

Sign-up and sign-in services.

Security features such as Multi-Factor Authentication (MFA) checks for compromised credentials, account takeover protection, and phone and email verification.

Social sign-in with Facebook, Google, and Login with Amazon, as well as sign-in with SAML identity providers from your user pool.

User directory management and user profiles.

Customized workflows and user migration through AWS Lambda triggers.

Option A is invalid because this would be a maintenance overhead.

Options B and D are invalid because these are not used to manage users.

217. **B** (Use AWS Lambda function to change the bucket ACL)

    D (Use AWS Config to monitor changes to the AWS Bucket)

Explanation:

Option A does not seem to be the most appropriate.

Option C is not valid because it is impossible to monitor changes in the AWS bucket using the Trusted Advisor API.

218. **C** (Create a new CloudTrail trail with one new S3 bucket to store the logs and with the global services option selected. Use IAM roles S3 bucket policies and Multi Factor Authentication (MFA) Delete on the S3 bucket that stores your logs.)

Explanation:

AWS Identity and Access Management (IAM) is integrated with AWS CloudTrail, a service that logs AWS events made by or on behalf of your AWS account. CloudTrail logs authenticated AWS API calls as well as AWS sign - in events and collects this event

information in Amazon S3 bucket files. You have to make sure all services are included. Option B is therefore partially correct.

Option D is invalid because you should ideally just create one S3 bucket.

Option B is invalid because you need to ensure that global services is select.

Option D is invalid because you should use bucket policies.

219. **A** ({

"Version":"2012-10-17"

"Id":"PutObj"

"Statement": [

{

"Sid":"DenyUploads",

"Effect":"Deny",

"Principal":"*",

"Action":"s3:PutObject",

"Resource":"arn:aws:s3:::demo/*",

"Condition":{

"StringNotEquals":{

"s3:x-amz-server-side-encryption":"aws-kms"

}

}

}

]

})

Explanation:

The condition of "s3:x-amz-server-side-encryption":"aws:kms" ensures that objects which are uploaded need to be encrypted.

Options B, C and D are invalid because you have to ensure that the condition of "s3:x-amz-server-side-encryption":"aws:kms" is present.

220. **C** (Use CloudTrail Log File Integrity Validation.)

Explanation:

You can use CloudTrail file integrity validation to determine whether a log file has been modified, deleted, or unchanged after it has been delivered by CloudTrail. This feature is built using industry standard algorithms: hashing SHA-256 and digital signing SHA-256 with RSA. This makes it computationally infeasible to modify, delete or forge CloudTrail log files without detection. You can use the AWS CLI to validate the files in the location where CloudTrail delivered them.

In security and forensic investigations, validated log files are invaluable. A validated log file, for example, allows you to positively assert that the log file itself has not changed, or that specific user credentials have performed specific API activity. The process of validating the integrity of the CloudTrail log file also lets you know whether a log file has been deleted or changed, or positively asserts that no log files have been delivered to your account over a given period of time.

Options A, B and D are invalid because log file integrity validation for CloudTrail logs needs to be checked.

221. **B** (The master key encrypts the cluster key. The cluster key encrypts the database key. The database key encrypts the data encryption keys.)

Explanation:

Amazon Redshift uses a key - based four - tier encryption architecture. The architecture is made up of keys for data encryption, a database key, a cluster key and a master key.

Data encryption keys encrypt the cluster's data blocks. A randomly - generated AES-256 key is assigned to each data block. These keys will be encrypted using the cluster database key.

The database key encrypts the cluster's data encryption keys. A randomly generated AES-256 key is the database key, which is stored on a disk in the network separately from Redshift - Cluster Amazon and is passed over a secure channel to this cluster.

The cluster key encrypts the database key for the Amazon Redshift cluster.

Option A is wrong, as the master key encrypts the cluster key and does not include the database key.

Option C is incorrect because the master key encrypts the cluster key and not the data encryption keys.

Option D is incorrect because the master key encrypts the cluster key only.

222. **D** (Assign an IAM Role and assign it to the EC2 Instance)

Explanation:

Options A, B and C are invalid because using users, groups or access keys is an invalid security practice when giving access to resources from other AWS resources.

223. **A** (Peer identity authentication between VPN gateway and customer gateway)

    C (Protection of data in transit over the Internet)

    E (Data integrity protection across the Internet)

    F (Data encryption across the Internet)

Explanation:

Option A is the right option. The implementation of VPN IPSec tunnel requires peer identity authentication between the VPN gateway and the customer gateway.

Option C is correct because it protects internet transit data.

Option E is correct- Integrity of internet - transmitted data can also be achieved through IPSec tunnel.

Option F is the right option. Data is encrypted which is transmitted through the IPSec tunnel.

IPSec is a widely adopted protocol that can be used to provide end to end protection for data.

Options B and D are invalid as there is no complete end - to - end encryption guarantee using IPSec.

224. **A** (Use EBS volume encryption)

    D (Use EBS volume replication)

Explanation:

Data stored in Amazon EBS volumes is stored redundantly in multiple physical locations as part of the normal operation of these services and free of charge. Amazon EBS replication is stored within the same availability zone, not over multiple zones, therefore, regular snapshots to Amazon S3 are highly recommended for long - term data durability. Amazon Data Lifecycle Manager (Amazon DLM) can be used to automate the creation, retention and deletion of snapshots taken for the backup of your Amazon EBS volumes.

You can be sure that snapshots are cleaned regularly with lifecycle management and that costs are kept under control.

A lifecycle policy consists of these core settings:

Schedule: Defines how often snapshots can be created and how many snapshots can be kept. The creation of snapshot begins within one hour of the specified starting time. If

the creation of a new snapshot exceeds the maximum number of snapshots, the oldest snapshot will be deleted.

Resource type—The AWS resources are managed by policies, in this case, EBS volumes.

Target tag—The tag that must be associated with an EBS volume for it to be managed by the policy.

Option A is correct. Encryption does ensure data durability.

Option D is the right option. To protect you from component failure, each Amazon EBS volume is replicated automatically within its Availability Zone, offering high availability and durability. But it does not have such an explicit feature.

225. **D** (Upload data to S3 and use lifecycle policies to move the data into Glacier for long-term archiving.)

Explanation:

For data archiving and long - term backup, Amazon Glacier is a secure, durable and extremely low - cost cloud storage service. Customers can reliably store large or small amounts of data for up to $ 0.004 per gigabyte per month; a substantial savings compared to on - site solutions.

You can create transition actions with Amazon lifecycle policies in which you define transition objects to another Amazon S3 storage class. For example, you can select transition objects to the storage class STANDARD IA (IA, for Infrequent Access) 30 days after creation, or archive objects to the storage class GLACIER one year after the creation.

Option A is invalid since IAM policies cannot be used to transfer data to Glacier.

Option B is invalid because lifecycle policies are not used to move data to Redshift.

Option C is invalid because EBS volumes are not subject to lifecycle policies.

226. **A** (Ensure that the HTTPS listener sends requests to the instances on port 443)

   B (Ensure that the load balancer listens on port 443)

Explanation:

You can create an HTTP (80) and HTTPS (443) ports load balancer. If you specify that the HTTPS listener sends requests on port 80 to the instances, the load balancer will terminate the requests and will not encrypt the load balancer communication to the instances. If the HTTPS listener sends requests on port 443 to the instances, communication is encrypted from the load balancer to the instances.

Option C is invalid because for the HTTPS listener you need to use port 443.

Option D is invalid because there is a need for secure traffic, so port 80 should not be used.

227. C (Use a Lambda authorizer)

Explanation:

An Amazon API Gateway Lambda authorizer (formerly known as a custom authorizer) is a Lambda function that you provide to control access to your API methods. A Lambda authorizer uses authentication strategies for the bearer token like OAuth or SAML. It may also use information described by headers, paths, query strings, stage variables, or context variables request parameters.

Options A, B and D are invalid as they cannot be used if custom authentication / authorization is required for calls to the API gateway.

228. D (Generate pre-signed URLs for each user as they request access to protected S3 content)

Explanation:

By default, all objects and buckets are private. If you want your user / customer to be able to upload a specific object to your bucket, the pre - signed URLs are useful, but you do not require AWS security credentials or permissions. When creating a pre - signed URL, you must provide your security credentials, specify a bucket name, an object key, an HTTP method (PUT to upload objects), and date and time of expiration. The pre - signed URLs are only valid for the duration specified.

Option A is invalid because this would be too difficult to implement at a user level.

Option B is invalid because this is not possible.

Option C is invalid because this is used for serving private content via CloudFront.

229. A (Use AWS Shield Advanced to protect the EC2 Instances)

Explanation:

Option C is invalid because this would take time and revenue loss is a big concern for the company.

Options B and D are invalid because they cannot be used to protect the instances.

230. A (Use AWS WAF to block the IP addresses)

Explanation:

AWS WAF used to protect Application Load Balancers and Cloud front in the following:

A web Access Control List (web ACL) allows you to control the web requests that your Amazon CloudFront distributions or Application Load Balancers respond to. The following types of requests can be allowed or blocked:

Contains a specified string or match a regular expression pattern (regex) in a specific part of requests.

Originates from a particular country or countries.

Originates from an IP address or a range of IP addresses.

Appears to contain malicious SQL code (known as SQL injection).

Appears to contain malicious scripts (known as cross-site scripting).

Exceeds a specified length.

Options B and C are invalid because these services cannot be used to block IP addresses.

Option D is invalid because by default Security Groups have the Deny policy.

231. **C** (Setup VPC peering between the central server VPC and each of the team's VPCs.)

Explanation:

A VPC peering connection is a network connection between two VPCs that allows you to use private IPv4 addresses or IPv6 addresses to route between them. Instances in either VPC can communicate as if they are in the same network. You can create a VPC peering connection between your own VPCs, or with a VPC in another AWS account within a single region.

Options A and B are invalid as VPC Peering is required.

Option D is invalid because VPC Peering is available

232. **A** (Enable MFA for these user accounts)

Explanation:

Enable Multi - Factor Authentication (MFA) for privileged IAM users (users allowed to access sensitive resources or APIs) for additional security. Users have a device with MFA that generates a unique authentication code (one - time password, or OTP). Users must provide their normal credentials (such as their user name and password) as well as the OTP. The MFA device can either be a special piece of hardware, or it can be a virtual device (such as running on a smartphone in an app).

233. **C** (Use the aws:Referer key in the condition clause for the bucket policy)

Explanation:

Restricting Access to a Specific HTTP Referrer.

Suppose you have a domain name of website (www.example.com or example.com) with links to photos and videos stored in the examplebucket of your S3. By default, all S3 resources are private, so they can only be accessed by the AWS account that created the resources. To allow read access from your website to these objects, you can add a bucket policy that allows with a condition s3:GetObject permission, using the aws: referer key that the get request must originate from specific webpages. The following policy specifies the StringLike condition with the aws:Referer condition key.

{

"Version":"2012-10-17"

  "Id":"http referer policy example",

  "Statement":[

{

"Sid":"Allow get requests originating from www.example.com and example.com.",

"Effect":"Allow",

"Principal":"*",

"Action":"s3:GetObject",

"Resource":"arn:aws:s3:::examplebucket/*",

"Condition":{

"StringLike":{"aws:Referer":["http://www.example.com/*","http://example.com/*"]}

}

}

]

}

Option A is invalid because aws:sites is not a valid condition key.

Option B is invalid because giving public access is not a secure way to provide access.

Option D is invalid because IAM roles will not be assigned to web sites.

234.   **A**   ("Effect":"Allow",   "Action":   ["aws-portal:ViewUsage,"   aws-portal:ViewBilling"],"Resource": "*")

Explanation:

Options B, C and D are invalid because the actions should be aws-portal:ViewUsage and aws-portal:ViewBilling.

235. **B** (Use separate AWS accounts for each of the environments)

Explanation:

Multiple accounts are recommended by AWS security for such type of setups.

Options A and C are invalid because it could become very difficult from a maintenance point of view.

Option D is partially valid, but having multiple accounts for this setup is a best practice.

236. **C** (Use TrueCrypt for EBS volumes on Linux instances)

    D (Use Windows bit locker for EBS volumes on Windows instances)

Explanation:

It is also possible to enable EBS encryption when creating the volume and not for existing volumes. Existing tools can be used for encryption at the OS level.

Option A is wrong. On launching an instance, you cannot choose to encrypt an unencrypted boot volume. Before launching, your custom AMI must have its boot volume encrypted before launch so that you cam have boot volumes encrypted.

Option B is wrong. AWS Systems Manager is a management service that helps you collect inventory of software automatically, apply OS patches, create system images, and configure operating systems for Windows and Linux.

237. **D** (CloudTrail, AWS Config, IAM Credential Reports)

Explanation:

You can use AWS CloudTrail to provide your account with a history of AWS API calls and related events. Calls made with the AWS Management Console, AWS Command Line Interface, AWS SDKs and other AWS services are included in this history.

Options A, B and C are invalid because it is required to ensure that you use the services of CloudTrail, AWS Config, and IAM Credential Reports.

AWS Config is a service that allows you to evaluate, audit and evaluate your AWS resources configurations. Config continuously monitors and records configurations of your AWS resource and allows you to automate evaluation of recorded configurations against desired configurations. With Config, you can review changes in configurations and relationships between AWS resources, dive into detailed resource configuration histories, and determine your overall compliance against the configurations specified in your internal guidelines. This enables you to simplify compliance auditing, security analysis, change management, and operational troubleshooting.

You can generate and download a credential report. That lists all the users on your account, including passwords and access keys, and MFA devices. An AWS Management Console, AWS SDKs, Command Line Tools, and the IAM API provides a credential report.

238. **A** (Ensure that UserB is given the right permissions in the Key policy)

Explanation:

Authentication and access control KMS API operations can be done through Key policies and IAM Policies.

In our scenario, we receive an error indicating that the "DescribeKey" action has not been authorized by UserB. It is because the key policy does not define this permission. Therefore, the correct option is A.

239. **B** (See CloudTrail for usage of the Customer Master Key)

   C (See who is assigned the permissions to the Customer Master Key)

Explanation

Direct way to see the key is to see the current access permissions and CloudTrail logs.

Examining CMK Permissions to Determine the Scope of Potential Usage'

Determining who or what currently has access to a Customer Master Key (CMK) may help you determine how widely the CMK has been used and if it is still needed. To learn how to determine who or what currently has access to CMK, go to Determining access to an AWS KMS Customer Master Key.

Examining AWS CloudTrail Logs to Determine Actual Usage

AWS KMS is integrated with AWS CloudTrail, so CloudTrail log files record all AWS KMS API activity. If you have CloudTrail switched on in the region where your Customer Master Key (CMK) is located, you can review your CloudTrail log files to view a history of all AWS KMS API activity for a specific CMK and its history of use. You may be able to use the history of the use of a CMK to help you determine if you still need it or not.

240. **B** (Use MFA on all users and accounts, especially on the root account.)

Explanation:

Multi - Factor Authentication can add to your AWS account an another layer of security. Even if you go to the dashboard for your security credentials, one item is to enable MFA on your root account.

About Our Products

Other products from IPSpecialist LTD regarding AWS technology are:

 AWS Certified Cloud Practitioner Technology Workbook

 AWS Certified Solution Architect - Associate Workbook

 AWS Certified Solution Architect - Professional Technology Workbook

 AWS Certified Developer Associate Technology Workbook

 AWS Certified DevOps Engineer - Professional Technology Workbook

 AWS Certified Advanced Networking – Specialty Technology Workbook

 AWS Certified Big Data – Specialty Technology Workbook

 AWS Certified Security – Specialty Technology Workbook

Upcoming products from IPSpecialist LTD regarding Cloud technology are:

 GCP Associate Cloud Engineer Technology Workbook

 GCP Professional Cloud Architect Technology Workbook

 GCP Professional Data Engineer Technology Workbook

Note from the Author:

Reviews are gold to authors! If you have enjoyed this book and it helped you along your certification, would you consider rating it and reviewing it?

Link to Product Page: